MW00627913

The Brady Keys, Jr. Story

"Overcoming Adversity
By Staying
Within The Blessing"

Latrina M. Patrick

The Brady Keys, Jr. Story

"Overcoming Adversity
By Staying
Within The Blessing"

Latrina M. Patrick

PUBLISHED BY:
THE KEYS GROUP
407 S. SLAPPEY BLVD.
ALBANY, GEORGIA 31701

Dedication

This book is for all the Keys Kids, the "bird heads" as I affectionately call them.

I thank God for a mother who prayed me to success. I thank God for a wife who tolerated my shortcomings, and contributed to my success. I thank my kids, sister-in-law and a great football team for their love and support.

I thank consultants, and a mother-in-law, business people and especially the Rooney family for their help. Thank you all.

But this book is dedicated to the Glory of God. God I hope you are glorified by this book. I could not live clean enough to truly glorify you. I hope this book inspires others to do it when people say, "you can't do this or you can't do that."

God, this book is a true testimony that you and only you have the last word.

Thank you for Divine Wisdom, Divine Understanding, and Divine Direction.

Contents

Chapter   *Page*

Part 1
The Early Years

1. The Power of Prayer 8

2. It Takes A Village 12

3. Like Father Like Son 15

4. Making A Dream A Reality 18

5. The Conflict Begins 23

6. Irreconcilable Differences 27

7. A Second Chance 29

8. Sights on Pittsburgh 32

Part 2
The Family

9. Pro-Football 37

10. The Strong Woman Behind the Man 42

11. My Father 46

12. Fatherhood 52

13. Lynn 55

14. The Boys 58

15. Yvette 64

Part 3
Taking It To The Next Level

16. Football to Finance 69

17. Football to Finance II 74

18. Wall Street 81

19. Farewell to Football 84

20. The Showdown 87

21. The Business of Business is Business 93

22. Move to the Motor City 97

23. If You Build Your Community, You Build Your Business . . 105

24. Keys Meets The Colonel 109

25. Albany, Georgia 113

26. A Rude Awakening 118

27. KAB & WJIZ - Divine Intervention 121

28. Acts of Faith 128

29. Moving Forward 130

30. Remembering Brady 136

31. Born Again 143

Brady's Bits 150

Epilogue 153

Brady Keys Journey To A Dream 159

Historical Photos 161

Photos 175

Part 1

The Early Years

Picture of A.C. when she was young.

Chapter 1

The Power of Prayer

"I had this child in marriage, and while his father did not want to marry me, he was forced to be his daddy. I knew once he and I were married and I got pregnant, he would not want a child because he was a big, famous athlete in Negro baseball at the time. I knew he would not stay with me and the child so I spent nine months in prayer for this young child. I prayed that he would be healthy while in the womb. I prayed that he would be healthy as a young child, but it didn't happen like that. God does not do things the way we do things. When you pray for things, Satan attacks, and he attacked my son. He was a very sickly child, but God provided for him even though we had no money, no food, no nothing. The people I worked for as a maid always gave me money for his health care so I was able to get the best of healthcare. I prayed that he would be a good little boy and not get into any trouble, but it didn't work out that way. He didn't get

into any big trouble, but he was fighting all the time, throwing rocks and hitting people all the time in cars, shooting people with his BB gun, terrorizing the neighborhood. But all of this did not deter him from being a good boy because he had a good heart, and he was forgiven by his friends, but he didn't do anything to anybody unless they did something to him over and over again, so this was a last resort. I prayed that he would be faithful because we would have meager means. This did not work out the way I prayed for it, but they did happen in God's way."—A.C.

Before he was even born, the life of Brady Keys, Jr., seemed to have been pre-destined to be a life of hardship and disappointment, but his mother, A.C., never accepted the unfortunate circumstances life had dealt her, and as a result she ensured that her son did not either. From the time she conceived young Brady, A.C. prayed that her child would have a good and prosperous life filled with love, hope, and success.

Brady Keys, Jr., was born into poverty in the ghetto of Austin, Texas. He was raised in a meager two bedroom house, but by today's standards it is difficult to call it a house. It could be more accurately described as a dreary, wood shack with no insulation or indoor plumbing. The two room structure was shared with the majority of his maternal extended family. Living in the house with him and his mother was also his Aunt Clara, her children Otis, Frank and Clarence; there was his Aunt Mary Jane and her two children, Wayne and Beverly; for a while there was his Aunt Roberta and her daughter Shirley, and son Junior. All of these people managed to share the same small roof and crowded quarters for years, and according to Brady they did so without any discord.

"That house with all those people, there was total peace. There were people all over one another, women without husbands, and children all over one another, and there was not so much as a peep of problems. We just lived together," Brady recalled.

He attributes most of the peace in their overcrowded home to the patriarch of the family, his 7 foot tall 400 pound grandfather, who they all feared. Although his grandfather rarely lived in the house with them, Brady said the remote possibility of his grandfather showing up was enough to keep the family in line.

"You feared your grandfather first, you respected him second, and you did what he said third, and believe it or not, he left out the word love. When my grandfather came, I ran, everybody ran. He wasn't fat, just a huge, huge, huge man. He beat, shot, threw at girls, so with that kind of terror, absolute terror, he terrorized the whole town, not just us. He shot at children, he shot at people, he beat people up, and he had at least three or four wives," Brady said.

Brady insists the family had an abundance of love, but not much else. The house was filled with women who were not working, and during this time there was no welfare and no jobs for anybody, but somehow they managed to survive. They ate syrup and bread most of the time, or sugar sandwiches, and on the best days they had beans and rice. Also, as a result of the family not having any money, the kids were forced to be creative. "We made our own toys, you had to use your imagination to make toys. We made them out of mud, bricks, trees; we made them out of things God gave us," Brady recalled.

It wasn't until Brady was 13 years old before he received his first bicycle, and he was in junior high school before he got his first pair of dress pants. Things other kids perceived as luxuries, were unfathomable to him. When most children had several pairs of shoes, he received one pair of sneakers a year, which he would stuff with paper once the soles wore out because he knew that his mother could not afford to buy him new ones.

Despite his life of poverty, Brady was able to see beyond his circumstances. At eight years old he made the announcement that set him on the path to his journey of success. One night during dinner Brady lifted his head from eating his meal, and said to his mother, "A.C. I'm going to be a professional football player, and a business man!" His mother looked at her ambitious son and said, "Son, if you say you want to be a football player, and a business man, then that is what you will be!" The other family members, who were present at dinner, gave him a skeptical look, and continued eating their meal. However, his mother never doubted her son, and from that day forward, she encouraged him to pursue his dream.

A.C.'s support of her ambitious son was unwavering, and every opportunity she had she would encourage his dream. "She never allowed a doubt to creep in, and she discounted everything anybody else would say to the contrary, and I began to discount it to. People are always telling me I can't do things, but I don't hear it. How can I hear it when I've heard from this woman that I could do it."

Brady on the left, with his friend Bo Collins at age 13 with first bicycle in background.

Chapter 2

It Takes A Village

The close proximity of the family created an environment of support, and everybody did what they had to do, especially when it came to taking care of each other. Brady recalls how independent they were of each other. "It was like an indian village. I was A.C.'s child, but that didn't mean anything. I was raised by a community of women. My childhood of extreme poverty was a total surrounding of love by women who took care of me, who took care of everybody else. Everybody took care of everybody else's kids."

Brady recalls how everybody did what they had to do without complaint. "I remember my Aunt Fannie Mae, and my older cousin Lawrence Brown. They didn't live there. Lawrence was about eight years older than the rest of us, and he was the idol. He worked from the time he was five years old; he took care of his mother who was sick, and when he was 13 years old he owned his first piece of land. He was the standard by which all of us strived. When he came around we worshiped this man because he was so brave, so strong. He was so smart, and so thrifty. In spite of working a full time, eight hour job from five years old, working all the way through school and college he took care of his mother."

Although there was strong family support within the small, overcrowded house, Brady was completely devoted to his mother, and in many cases he was admittedly selfish with her time. "I was a very selfish little boy. I had my mother and I did not want anybody to be around my mother. I had no brothers and sisters. I was basically selfish with her, but I was generous with everything else."

Because of the close relationship with his mother, and the lack of a father figure, Brady was sometimes very challenging for his mother to deal with. Much like he is today, Brady was a stubborn child, so stubborn he wouldn't address his mother as such, but instead he called her by her first name, A.C. "I was a strong baby, and she had to do certain things to get me to do things. I would take a whipping if I didn't want to do something, and you just can't beat a baby up all the time, so she had to figure out ways to get me to do things. That's the kind of child I was, I was just stubborn. I knew what I wanted, and I would not accept anything else."

When he was only six years old, A.C. knew Brady was going to be more than a handful to handle. Brady recalled an incident that was indicative of how stubborn and independent he was even as a young boy. "My mother went out to eat dinner one day with her boyfriend who became her husband, my stepfather named Garland. First of all, when they went to eat they were smooching and talking and having fun, and they put the whole chicken on the table, and I ate the whole chicken while it was sitting there. On the way back home, in a T-model Ford, I was leaning on the door and fell out the car. They left me there, they didn't even know I had fallen out. They had driven 10 miles and when I fell out, I sat right there in the street, and I would not move."

When A.C returned home she was questioned by her mother about Brady's whereabouts, and when she did not know where he was, "my grandmother beat my mother and told her she was going to beat her until she went back to get me. She said she was not going back to get me because I had eaten all the chicken, and complained that I had been grouchy and fussy. So my grandmother said she was going to whip her until I came home."

In the meantime, while A.C. was being punished, Brady's Aunt Maryanne decided to go out to find him. "When they came and found me I was sitting there, and when they got there I said I'm not getting up from here. I said "A.C. has to come back and pick me up, and I'm not going to move until she gets back." They said, "Your mama is getting a whipping until you get back, and I'm going to whip you until you get there." She whipped me until I got back, and when I got back my mama whipped me," Brady laughs as he remembered.

He fondly remembers the feeling of love he felt from the women in his household who all had a role in raising him. "I was raised by a community of women, and the love of those women is why women are all around me today. Everywhere I go there are nothing but women. That's why women like me so much because I know how to relate to women."

Brady in front of the house where he was reared. 1912 East 21st, Austin, Texas.

I thank God for these humble beginnings. He blessed me with nothing (materially). Therefore, I don't place my value in material things ... rather in spiritual things. Thank you Lord!

Brady Keys Sr.

Chapter 3

Like Father Like Son

Brady Keys, Sr., had minimal to zero involvement in the life and rearing of his son. After his shotgun wedding to A.C., he literally abandoned her, and their child. But according to Brady, Jr., he never missed the presence of his father until he was in his teenage years. He also believes had his father had an active role in his life, he probably would not be the success he is today.

"God knew what he was doing. Everything my mother prayed for me to do, my father would have undone. My father had the wrong idea about life. The day I was born he left and said I don't want anything to do with this. It had nothing to do with whether I was his or not, he just did not want the responsibility. He raised a whole bunch of kids, and the jury is out as to how many are going to be successful."

Even though Brady, Sr., abandoned Brady, Jr., and A.C. he

My father had three kids by other women. Jackie (sister, not shown) and two brothers Brain and Kenny who live in Los Angeles.

went on to remarry and eventually have more kids with whom he had an active role in raising. Brady, Jr., has a half sister, Jackie, and two half brothers, Kenny and Brian. Unlike Brady, his siblings were raised in a traditional household with a mother and a father. In Brady's opinion, his siblings were extremely protected and sheltered by their father, and he attributes that to his father over compensating for the mistake he made when he abandoned Brady, Jr., and A.C.

As a young boy Brady never felt the absence of his father, but he admits to feeling curious about him prior to his adolescent years. "I didn't see my father until I was ten. It was my wish, but my mother did not encourage it because she was afraid I would be hurt."

His curiosity about his father began to get the best of him so he ventured out on his own to see him. "At ten I snuck around to somebody's house and I acted like I was playing, and everybody walked out and said, "there he is out there, he just wants to see you," and that was the truth."

Brady was very easy to recognize because he was the spitting image of his father. His attempt to see his father was successful, but brief. "I spent about an hour with my father and that was it," Brady recalled.

After the brief meeting with his father at age ten, Brady once again began to feel his father's absence when he became a teenager. "When I became 15 I went through the I want to spend some time phase. Fifteen is when male children need and yearn for a father, and if one does not exist then there is a void that something fills, and it's usually crime. At fifteen that void appeared and I needed to see my father."

Surprisingly, without the influence of his father, Brady shared several common interests with him, the main interest being the love of sports. Brady, Sr., was a great athlete before his time. He was a professional athlete in the Negro Baseball League. This common interest and love of sports was what eventually brought the two together.

"At 16 I had played a year of football, and I had already become somewhat a renowned athlete at a young age myself, so my father wanted to see me. I went to San Francisco to spend the summer with him, my brother Kenny, my sister Jackie, and his wife Margaret in their luxurious house, and their new car."

Not long after he arrived to spend the summer with his father, Brady began to feel cheated from a life with his father, a life his father had refused to give him, but gave freely to Kenny and Jackie. He couldn't see it then, but in retrospect he believes it was to his advantage that he grew up without the influence of his father.

"I didn't know how much a blessing it was not to have my father's influence. My brother Kenny was a spoiled brat crying all the time, and he was really not able to cope with life. Jackie was able to cope. She made it through the maze of spoilness."

Brady also said he believes his father spoiled his children because he wanted to make sure he didn't reject any more of his children as he had rejected him.

The common interest of sports brought his father to him, but as Brady's career began to blossom in professional sports he said his father once again became distant and somewhat resentful.

Chapter 4

Making A Dream A Reality

As Brady became older he began to take the necessary steps to make his childhood dream become a reality. At age eight he proclaimed that he wanted to become a professional football player, so he began to play football, and he set a goal to make the team once he entered junior high school.

Upon entering Kealing Junior High School, Brady tried out for varsity football. His mother thought her son was too small, and too young to play football. She couldn't bare the thought of all those big boys piling up on her baby. In an effort to protect him, she encouraged him to pursue one of his other interests, playing the saxophone. She knew he loved to play his cousin Lena's boyfriend's saxophone when he went to visit her. One day after returning home from school, he found a surprise awaiting him - a brand new saxophone. However, his mother's plan was unsuccessful because Brady played that saxophone twice before he told his mother, "I don't want to play this, I want to play football." His mother returned the saxophone, and Brady was able to do what he loved most - play football.

The only thing Brady ever really wanted to do was to play football, but he would soon discover that he would be constantly confronted with many challenges, and obstacles that would make it difficult to make his dream a reality.

One of his first obstacles was a diagnosis from the school athletic physician, Dr. Washington, who warned Brady about his bad heart. But Brady refused to believe the doctor's diagnosis. He played a variety of sports for years without an incident, but if the doctor was right with his diagnosis, Brady's career would be over before it began.

Brady couldn't imagine his life without football. He felt something had to be done, so he took it upon himself to change the doctor's report before giving it to the athletic office.

Every morning for two weeks Brady was up before dawn. He jogged five miles everyday before walking two miles to school. His training schedule was rigorous, but he was determined to fulfill his dream, and make the team.

He made the team, and finally the day arrived for Brady to play. Although he wasn't on the varsity team, he was thrilled to be playing football. They lined up for the kickoff. The big boys on the varsity team gritted their teeth, and made faces at the B-team. The whistle sounded, shoe leather sounded against the teed up ball, and suddenly 22 charged up players sped toward contact. The ball soared 55 yards before settling into Brady's arms. He took off in a flash, evading two huge varsity defensive backs at his own 35 yard line, then he sprung free of the others with a burst of speed at midfield.

Coach Crawford looked on in disbelief, a mean pair of varsity mates closed in on Brady at the varsity 25 yard line. Rotating the ball to his left hand, Brady's stiff arm caught one pursuer off balance, and flattened him at the 16 yard line. Brady was unable to fully recover top speed before the other man overtook him, and cut him down at the varsity 9.

In a rage, Coach Crawford grabbed a long paddle, and yelled at the varsity team to line up midfield. "You no-tackling babies! You spineless jackasses! You let a little thirteen year old child run right through you, the length of the field like a damn jackrabbit! I'm going to take it out on your hides!

Billy Owens, the varsity captain argued, "Coach, that Keys kid has a reputation for being fast and tricky."

"Shut up. Just shut up, and give me your butts," Crawford shouted. Every player that received a paddling cursed the coach and that Keys kid.

"The little punk. He thinks he's really tough. Well, we'll fix him, we've got to show him who's boss," Owens vowed.

They lined up for the second kickoff. The varsity defense was not as confident. All eyes followed Brady as he moved to the B-team's 5 yard line. The ball was kicked, and Brady positioned himself at his 10 yard line as the varsity team came downfield. He moved left, then right, then he took off up the middle. Leaping over flattened blockers he tore through a tangle of tacklers and was free at midfield.

At the varsity 45, Brady tricked one player, pulled free of a second, and tried to evade a third when he was grabbed from behind by Captain Owens. Suddenly, he was hit from both sides, and he disappeared under the dead weight of two husky varsity tacklers. The varsity members gloated as Brady laid sprawled over the field.

Coach Crawford watched Brady for a moment, and then instructed him to go home, get some rest, and return the following day ready for practice.

Brady in his first football uniform in Austin, Texas.

Thirteen year old Brady waited anxiously in the end zone for the ball to come down. He had never seen a ball kicked so high in the air. He squinted his eyes from the sun as he looked up and waited and waited. "Hurry up ball!" he begged.

There was a deafening silence as the ball floated lazily in the air towards him. Everything around him appeared to be still. He felt alone and with all his thoughts to his self. This was his first time playing organized football. He had not known much about the game out of his neighborhood where he played pick-up games on a field full of rocks and broken glass.

Brady could feel the opposing team bearing down on him. Three of the boys on the kick-off team were over 19 years of age. One of them, it was rumored had just gotten out of jail. This did not phase Brady because he knew they were put out there to play for some purpose.

"Come down ball!" he demanded. Some how Brady knew that he would excel at football and that this game would take him places.

The ball finally came down deep in the end zone. Brady snatched the ball out of the air and took off down field ignoring his teammates waving at him to stay in the end zone.

Run Brady run!

SCHOOL DAYS 1950-'51
Kealing Jr. High

21

1953 — Brady making a 65 yard Touchdown run against Belmont High School. Polytechnic High vs. Belmont. Brady is wearing the number 38.

Brady with his first Football High School letter. He later made All-American in football, baseball and track.

Chapter 5

The Conflict Begins

Brady inevitably made the varsity team, and things began to look up for him as he began to make a name for himself in sports. However, shortly afterwards, unforeseen problems forced his family to relocate from Texas to Los Angeles.

"My family moved from Texas because my stepfather, Garland Franklin, was run out of town by some white folks in Texas. During those days it was common for White folks to plant drugs on Black people. The cops would plant things, and they planted something, I can't remember what it was because I was young at the time. They told him they would give him 24 hours to get out of town, and in 24 hours my mother and him had to leave. They left me there because the police was going to put him in prison. They didn't wait 24 hours, they left in seven hours."

Mother A.C. and step-father Garland before white cops ran Garland out of town.

Since that occurred in February, his mother allowed him to remain in Texas to complete the school semester before he joined his mother in California. He attended Polytechnic High School, and it didn't take long before he'd made a name for himself in football, just as he had done in Texas.

After a successful first year at Polytechnic, Brady's football career was threatened. He suffered an injury to his knee when he and some of his friends were playing high jump on a running track. He jumped the bar with no problem, but unfortunately he landed wrong and ripped the cartilage in his knee.

Brady ignored the pain in his knee joint until he no longer could. One day he tried to play football, and his knee locked up on him, and it sent him tumbling to the ground.

His mother couldn't afford the cost of surgery, so his teachers, along with the Polytechnic student body, raised money for his $3,000 operation. As soon as the money was raised, he was taken to UCLA for medical treatment. The specialists prognosis was highly unfavorable. He not only feared that Brady may never return to football, but he feared Brady would never walk again.

Miraculously, eleven days after the operation, and in direct conflict with the doctors predictions. Brady was up walking. One week later he played football on the delicate knee joint, but his premature return to football made his recovery long, and painful.

Brady was not only athletically gifted in football, but in other sports as well. He became a four sport sensation at Polytechnic. As a result, when his high school career began to come to an end, Brady began to receive scholarship offers from several different areas of sports outside of football.

He declined a $10,000 Brooklyn Dodgers offer to play professional baseball. He also had scholarship offers from over 75 colleges, including the University of Southern California (USC), and the University of California at Los Angeles, (UCLA). It was predicted that Brady was going to be an extraordinary football player.

USC sent one of their alumni, Walter D. Thomas, to try to persuade Brady to accept their offer.

Brady and Walter developed a very special relationship. Brady revered Walter. For the first time in his life he believed he had someone he could lean on. Walter was equally impressed with Brady, especially by Brady's athletic abilities. He wanted Brady to excel both athletically and academically.

He urged Brady to accept the offer from USC, and to secure his future after his football career ended. He encouraged Brady to learn about business. Walter believed that fame on a team like the USC Trojans, who were known nationally, could afford Brady the opportunity to make the perfect transition from football to the business arena. However, Brady rejected Walter's advice, and the offer to USC.

Brady wanted to accept the offer from UCLA, but his grades were inadequate. In an attempt to meet UCLA's entrance requirements, Brady enrolled at East Los Angeles Junior

Brady at Poly High with an injured left knee.

College. He hoped to bring his grades up, and later transfer to
UCLA. Unfortunately, Brady became distracted, and his aca-
demic efforts began to slack. He had every opportunity to excel
academically. He had a tutor, a car from UCLA, and from USC,
he had clothes and money. He could have done it, but he allowed
himself to lose focus. Rather than study, he chose to spend time
with his lady friend, Delores Ward, and/or sit in the student
union, and listen to the jokes of Richard Pryor. As a result of his
lack of focus and attention to his studies, Brady dropped out of
school, and he married Delores.

Chapter 6

Irreconcilable Differences

The impetuous decision to marry soon became a regretful decision. Not long after their nuptials, Brady and Delores began to realize what a mistake they had made. "Our marriage was stormy and unhappy. We fought all the time. Delores was head strong, and damn right contentious. She was pregnant with Tyrone when we said "I do". When she went into the hospital to birth Tyrone I named him, Brady Keys, III. Well, when I left the hospital, she changed his name to Brady Tyrone Keys, and even signed my name to the document. She always took it upon herself to make changes without my consent. She wasn't a team player. Eventually, the fights between us became more frequent, and violent."

Brady and Delores' marriage lasted for about two years, but as the marriage came to an end, they found out they were expecting another baby. Their second child was a little girl, whom Brady named Yvette.

"I had no idea of the impact, and the emotional strain the divorce would have on me. I loved my children dearly, that was the only common interest left that Delores and I shared."

Brady said he contemplated saving the marriage for the sake of the children, he felt the cost was too high, so the couple divorced. Delores took everything Brady owned with the exception of his car, the clothes on his back, his mattress and his box springs. He was back to zero again.

He moved into an apartment on 23rd street in Los Angeles, where he had to start all over from scratch. The divorce left him with hefty child support payments. He began working three jobs, two 8 hour jobs, and one 4 hour part-time job. He slept only when he gave out from exhaustion, or extreme fatigue. This pattern continued for months. He felt he was fading, but the thought of his kids not having their basic needs met, drove him on and on.

In the midst of working, he noticed the most beautiful lady he had ever seen. She was standing in the doorway of the apartment below his. He could not breathe when he saw her. He was so taken with her that he would pull the curtains back to watch her every morning as she left for work. Being the connoisseur that he was, he felt he just had to have her, so he tricked her into going out with him. She was sixteen, and really naive, and that was just the beginning.

"She was so sweet. It didn't take long for me to fall madly in love with Anna. She made the pain of my divorce less stressful. Without her support I don't know how I would have made it. I couldn't let her get away from me."

1954 — Brady "broad juming" 23'1" to set a school record for Poly High, after having a serious knee operation and the doctor saying he would never play sports again.

Chapter 7

A Second Chance

After a brief departure from football, Brady's passion, and love for football eventually inspired him to return to the game. He joined the Eagle Rock Athletic Club, a semi-professional unit.

Initially, Brady was discouraged because he was playing behind ex-All Americans Aramis Dandoy and Addison Hawthorne, who were both former USC starters. His attitude changed after he was moved up to be the key back, ahead of Dandoy and Hawthorne. He contemplated going to Canada the next season to star in the Canadian Football League.

While Brady was thinking about Canada, the Los Angeles Rams arranged a three team double-header at the Rose Bowl as the lid-lifter for the 1958 season. During the first half, the Rams played the Eagle Rock eleven; during the second half, another team.

Brady had an outstanding game. He carried ten times for more than 100 yards. A scout at the game, Fido Murphy of the Pittsburgh Steelers, asked Brady to sign with the Steelers as a member of the taxi squad. Brady felt insulted by the offer, and refused it. However, Murphy was undeterred by his refusal. Later, he offered Brady the chance to attend Colorado State University until he could be legally drafted as a free agent.

This idea was appealing to 21-year-old Brady who now felt he was ready to settle down. He had fallen in love with Anna, so he accepted the offer to Colorado State University, married Anna, and they moved to Colorado.

It became very difficult for Brady to be apart from Tyrone and Yvette. He didn't want them to grow up as he had without a father. The first year of marriage was extremely tough for Brady and Anna. Because they barely had any money, Brady hunted and fished so they could eat.

"It was a very difficult time for us in the beginning. Anna paid my child support for Tyrone and Yvette, and most of my college finances. I received a scholarship to attend Colorado State University, after turning down a chance to play semi-professional football in Canada. So off to Fort Collins, Colorado Anna and I went on a wing and a prayer. Our furniture was donated by my sister-in-law, Doris Mills. We were poor, but happy!"

With Brady in school and playing football, the only income they had was what Anna brought home from her $1.65 an hour cafeteria job at the university. Her salary wasn't much, but it allowed them to pay all of their living expenses, and child support, which Delores kept increasing.

"What makes a woman so bitter, so vindictive that she would do anything for revenge, including hurting an innocent baby. Delores was obsessed with malice towards not only me, but with Anna as well. In Delores' defense she probably had good reason to be mad as hell … but not to the extent you harm a person's child. You see, when my son Rodney was born he suffered with eye and foot problems.

I was playing professional football, and Delores filed suit against me claiming that not only had I failed to make the required child support payments, but the money in which she received was insufficient to support the needs of the children. Well, there was an immediate lien against all of my income. My son was five months premature and he required special medical care. I pleaded with Delores to release some of my money so that Rodney could be taken care of … she flatly refused.

The insurance did not cover all the medical expenses. When the day came for our baby to be released from the hospital, we had no money for his bills. Our baby stayed there for five days until we raised enough money to bring him home. This was brutal. It tore my wife apart! All those years, not months, but years Anna had support-ed her children. Anna financially supported Tyrone and Yvette, and never to this day has she ever made mention of it. The whole ugly affair did cause some strain between Anna and the children, but she never let it get in the way of what had to be done.

30

Brady with Eagle Rock coach and All-American Aramis Dandoy.

Chapter 8

Sights on Pittsburgh

Brady finally had his day to try out for a position on the Pittsburgh Steelers team. The environment was tense. The veteran players carefully watched and sized up the nine Black rookies that stood midfield in the hot July sun.

Everyone wanted to know how many of the nine rookies would actually make the team. They watched Assistant Coach Mike Nixon test #26 - Brady Keys, Jr. Coach Buddy Parker, who had been a star halfback for the 1935 NFL championship team the Detroit Lions, was impressed with Brady's style.

After five days passed, and six Black rookies had been eliminated, Brady remained with the team. He had one objective - to drive somebody OUT of the starting Steelers backfield position so he could take over.

The Steelers played their first exhibition season against the Baltimore Colts in Roanoke, Va., Brady was excited. He was a member of the kicking and receiving teams on kickoffs. The Baltimore coaching staff was aware of his reputation for held length kickoff and punt returns, and they prepared their strategy with that in mind. Brady was extremely disappointed when they intentionally kicked to Bill Butler, who had been on the Steeler team for three years.

The Colts had kicked to Butler three times, and Brady led the downfield charge as Butler's blocker. Brady was angry that Butler was stealing his thunder because he wanted to dazzle the Colts with a 100 yard scamper. He felt Butler was monopolizing the kickoffs. Brady became infuriated, he jumped up from the bench, grabbed Butler, and challenged him to "Get it on."

The other players were stunned by this rookie's behavior because Brady was challenging the star. Brady had to be restrained. Fortunately, Coach Parker was a tolerant man. He told Brady, "Don't worry boy, you'll get the opportunity to show this ball club what you can do."

It was during the second exhibition game against the Detroit Lions that Brady would face the second obstacle attempting to prevent him from fulfilling his childhood dream.

Brady confidently accepted the opening kickoff at the Steelers 10 yard line. As he ran along the eastern sideline, he could feel the surge of electricity that shot through him as he dashed toward the Steelers' 35. He leaped over charging bodies, but while in mid air someone hit his foot. He lost his balance, and fell on his back. Lucius Jackson, a lineman for the Lions, stumbled over Brady and collapsed the flimsy single ribbed protector. A pointed cleat from Jackson's shoe rammed into Brady's unprotected right eye drilling deep into his head, and also fracturing his nose.

Instantly, blood spewed from his eye, which caused excruciating pain. And as he bled from his nostrils, Brady screamed out, "I can't see! My God, Help me, I can't see!

In the darkness, Brady relived that horrific moment. He fingered the bandages that layered his head. "Why did this have to happen," he thought. Brady had been consumed with self-pity since the accident, but one day while lying in his bed something happened. He experienced a revelation, at that moment he firmly believed in Jesus Christ, and he suddenly realized that things don't just happen, but instead there is a specific reason why certain things happen to certain people.

He'd wanted to play professional football since he was eight years old, but since then he had been plagued by injuries. Now he wondered if he'd placed too much emphasis on football, and if perhaps there wasn't something else he was intended to do with his life. He also wondered if this was God's way of showing him that he had a higher calling.

This caused Brady to do a lot of soul searching because he knew this would be a defining moment in his life. He talked to his mother and found out that she also had visions of him doing something great that would affect a lot of people. This entire ordeal was frightening to Brady, because not only had an injury of this kind never occurred in Pittsburgh, but the surgical procedure that was needed to correct his problem was "experimental", and the doctor's couldn't guarantee a successful outcome.

A patch was inserted behind his eye in order to repair it. Brady underwent delicate surgery that allowed a short thread to be suspended from his nose, propping up the damaged eye. After two weeks of intensive testing the team of doctor's were ready to remove the patch from Brady's eye by pulling the thread. This critical, life changing moment was at hand, and Brady was scared. The doctor pulled the thread very quickly, and immediately Brady's face was covered with blood. In shock, he ran from the room, leaving everyone behind. The hospital was alerted of his critical situation and it was said that if Brady wasn't brought back immediately, he could bleed to death.

The hospital staff assumed he'd left the building, but unbeknownst to them, he'd actually passed out in the hospital from the excessive loss of blood.

Once again God interceded, five hours later, Brady woke up with dried blood on his face. He looked in the mirror, and he saw his reflection with perfect 20/20 vision.

**Anna and sister Doris Mills, left, two strong women amongst
many who have helped me.**

Nine Steeler Rookies 1961

Brady Keys is number 26. Len Burnett, 86, Brady's best friend and close business partner. They were the only two black players to make the team.

Chapter 9

Pro-Football

Of the nine Black rookies that started for Pittsburgh, Brady and Len Burnett were the only two remaining. During the opening game between the Steelers and the Giants, Coach Parker decided to see how Brady performed as back-up man for Tom Tracy, who was the starting backfield on the team.

Signaled to run a strong side, off tackle weave, Brady took the handoff from Bobby Layne, and then he noticed that the left side members of the Giants' defensive frontal had shed the Steelers blockers, and were crossing the scrimmage line. Brady was sure he wouldn't get anything on their side, so he reversed his field and pulled himself free of Andy Robustelli, the Giant's right end. He angled outside for a 22 yard pickup. It was the first down for Pittsburgh at New York's 46 yard line.

On his way back to the Steelers' huddle Brady felt a sense of pride for his first down carry. He was surprised when Tracy tapped him to take his position in the huddle along with Johnson, Bobby Layne, and Flanker. This confused Brady, so he went back to the bench.

When he returned to the bench Coach Parker was livid. "Boy, you'll never run another offensive play on this team as long as I'm coach," he yelled. Get one thing straight. NOBODY runs a reverse-field option on me.

After his run in with Parker, Brady worried that his career was finished before he ever really got started. However, a week later fate stepped in, and Brady was given another opportunity to shine. Burnett suffered a knee injury, and Captain Dean Derby couldn't keep up with the speeding receivers, so Parker moved Brady into Burnett's cornerback position.

Moving Brady into Burnett's position turned out to be a smart decision because Sample and Keys worked well together.

They were exceptionally fast, and they were both excellent open field runners with great footwork. They were also outstanding on punt returns, and they could carry interceptions the length of a gridiron across enemy goal lines. Brady adopted Sample's style and he took heed to Sample's advice.

"Talk tough. Hard hitting and loud talking will force the pros to respect you," Sample said.

In December of 1962, the president of the Steelers, Art Rooney, Sr., flew with the team to Washington, D.C. for the final game of the season. At this time, very few professional teams had better prospects than the Steelers, and nobody was more aware of that than Coach Parker. Parker had resigned as head coach of the Detroit Lions in 1958. At the time of his resignation, the Lions were the champions of the NFL.

Parker had spent five long years trying to catapult the Steelers into a contender with a 9-5 win loss record in 1962. They were the only Steelers team to win that many games in 37 seasons of NFL play. Since November his team had become formidable opponents.

Parker knew he had constructed an awesome team, and this particular year he felt the Eastern Division title was a strong possibility. They beat the Redskins, but they lost to Detroit in the Playoff Bowl. This defeat did not deter Parker from striving for the Eastern Division.

Two weeks after the Playoff Bowl loss, Big Daddy Lipscomb's performance in the Super Bowl made the '63 season even more feasible. The fans adored Lipscomb, and whenever he exited the field during the last quarter, they would give homage to him with a standing ovation.

In May 1963, the Steelers were devastated by the tragic news of Lipscomb's untimely death. After his demise, the Steelers had a streak of bad luck. By September of that same year, the Steelers had changed their course. They came away from the opening game of the 63 season against the Giants with renewed confidence. They crushed the Giants 31-0.

Brady was extremely aggressive during that game, he decided to take Sample's advice and talk tough. For the next three games their winning streak continued, until John Henry Johnson's game was temporarily ended by an ankle sprain. As a result of his sprained ankle, Johnson had to miss the next five games. With the records Johnson had set on the team, 1,151 net yards on 251 attempts in 1962, it was impossible for the Steelers to continue to win with two major losses in one year. First the loss of Lipscomb, and now the five game loss of Johnson.

Johnson returned in November just in time for their game against Cleveland. Upon his return, Brady predicted, "With John Henry ready, we'll beat the Browns like breaking sticks."

Brady and Clendenon Thomas had decided that the best way for them to handle the Cleveland Browns was to put Jim Brown out of the game by tearing into him on virtually every play. Brown was a tough opponent. He was six foot two and 228 pounds.

Brady and Thomas' plan had some glitches that manifested around the third quarter at Cleveland's 43 yard line. Brady noted that Brown had telegraphed his moves by glancing at the intended area of attack just before the snap of the ball. When the Browns came out of the huddle, and Frank Ryan began sounding signals, Brady warned his middle linebacker, 'Watch Brown, right up the middle."

Ryan handed off to Brown on an option thrust, inside or outside of Leo Cordileone's right tackle spot. Behind sharp blocking, Brown tore through the Steelers, past the middle linebacker, and into the open field. Thomas charged forward, and Brady took aim at Brown from Pittsburgh's right side, avoiding a head collision. Thomas developed towards his left for a side shot.

Brady now had a clear shot at Brown. At the last second, as Brady was about to throw a vicious elbow at him, Jim and Brady exchanged hard looks. Switching from the elbow throwing tactic, Brady jammed his shoulder against Brown's body, exposing his rib cage to Brown's fist as Thomas ran headlong into the two of them at Pittsburgh's 31 yard line. Trainers and water boys were scattered as the 3 men tumbled violently from the field of play onto the side lines. Clendenon was carried off the field. Keys and Brown got up painfully. Brady was bleeding from the mouth, nose, and both ears. Brown walked over to his teammates, seemingly unscathed, with only a minor wrist injury. The doctors stopped the bleeding, but Brady was unaware that he had fractured several ribs and ruptured a blood vessel, so he continued to play.

Brady continued to bleed for the remainder of the game. That remarkable play saved Pittsburgh, but for Brady, it was the end of his season. As a matter of fact, his injuries were not properly identified or treated until five months later.

Nonetheless, with Johnson back Coach Parker held onto his hopes for the Eastern Division title. The Steelers defeated the Cowboys 24-19. Before their final game of the season against the Giants their record was 7-3-3 and .700.

In their final games against the Giants, the Steelers saw the death of their hopes with a loss of 33-17. Many Steeler fans, and the late owner Art Rooney, Sr., say if Brady had been there to 'shut out' wide receiver Del Shofner of the Giants, as he had always done, the Steeler's would have gone to the Super Bowl.

Serious Brady Keys on the field in a Steeler's game against Dallas. The Steelers won.

Part 2

The Family

Brady and Anna Keys

Chapter 10

The Strong Woman Behind the Man

Being the wife of a multimillionaire would seem to be an enviable position, but it's a position that comes with its share of ups and downs. It's also a position where the prerequisites include class, dignity, and above all else ... trust and patience. All character traits that Anna Keys possesses, or has acquired during her marriage to Brady Keys, Jr.

"Brady and I lived in the same apartment complex when we met. He lived upstairs, I lived downstairs. We just stumbled into each other one day. I really didn't pay much attention to him at first. Time went by, and he began coming around making small talk. He would invite me to watch him play football. To tell you the truth, I really didn't think his football career would lead to much. Boy was I wrong!

When we got married I was only nineteen. I had a little job

working in a cafeteria. We were poor, but we were HAPPY! His football career didn't take off until later, much later. When I met Brady he didn't have anything. All that the Keys family has today is because He and I worked together to make it happen.

It was hard, hard work. I remember we didn't even have money to buy any furniture for our home. My mother and sister sent us second hand furniture, and we were very pleased. At least we had a place to sit down and eat."

Brady recalls that money has never been an issue for Anna. "Money is not a thing with her, it didn't matter to her. Everybody else could go on a date and they'd be paying for their girlfriends, and I'd go on a date and Anna would be paying my way because I had no money. I had nothing, but it wasn't a big deal with her. Of course I tease her about that now, I say I was pimping her."

After 38 years of marriage, Brady and Anna have come a long way from the young couple they once were with no furniture, food or money. When they were first married they had no money, but they had each other. They now have more than enough money, but they don't have the luxury of spending as much time together as they once did. This adjustment was difficult for Anna in the beginning, especially having to share her husband with so many other people who require his time and attention, but with time she says she has adapted.

"It use to be very difficult, but I'm older now, and I kind of accept everything. I sometimes wish my husband would spend more time at home with me. I'm looking forward to the day when it will be he and I, but it doesn't seem like that day will ever come. I guess I'm kind of selfish when it comes to my husband. It's always somebody out there that needs help, and Brady is always out there trying to help everybody. He'll leave me to go and help somebody else!

I used to get very upset because he kept such late, late, hours. I couldn't help but wonder if maybe he was seeing another woman. That was a long time ago. Time has a way of mellowing out a person. When you have been with the same man as long as I have, you don't worry about it. If he was going anywhere he would have left a long time ago. I cannot spend my time worrying about other

43

women. I'm kind of busy doing other things, and I just don't have time to sit at home waiting for him to come. I'm involved with most of my grandchildren, especially the one who lives with us. She's in high school now, so I'm involved with all the things she is doing, taking her here and there, and going to all the functions she's in, and helping out with other ones. When they need me I'm always there, so I don't have a problem with that anymore. I've just learned to give it to Jesus, and go ahead with my life."

Brady said Anna's behavior with the grandchildren is history repeating itself from when she spent the first 20 years of the business raising their children. "Exactly what she does now, it's just a repeat of the same situation. She's at more events than anybody."

Anna was so committed to the development of her children and raising them properly, that she didn't even contemplate going to work until they were all in school. Brady gives her all the credit for how well the children have turned out. He credits her with their good upbringing, especially since he was away a lot on business. Although he still had an active role in the lives of the children, he says Anna played a pivotal role in executing his wishes for the children and how they were raised.

"I give the orders and I set the standards and the policy with her and the children, but even though I may be the roughest and the toughest and the best, it takes a woman to carry out those things. It takes a strong woman, a caring woman to carry out your orders, and that is what Anna basically did, "he said.

Once the kids were raised and in school, Anna decided to go to work. "She did not get involved with the business until the last kid was in school about six months, she got bored. She had never worked and I brought her in. She was afraid so I told her to just answer the phone. She did that for 3-4 hours a day, and that went to full time," Brady recalled.

Anna eventually became more comfortable with her job and she began to escalate within the company. "She went from answering the phone to what it is now, she is a full fledged accounts payable accountant, all made on the job. She has been there for about 12 years now."

Her escalation within the company has still never changed her role in the company as it relates to getting involved with the day to day operation and decision making for the company. Brady insists that she has never had an interest in getting involved any further than she does. "In the 12 years she has been in the business, and in our levels of interest there is just a gap between us. She is bookkeeping and I am making giant deals. I never discuss anything with her. Even with the kids, we always talk about what they are concerned about, but not with all my business problems. She and the children have always been sheltered. I have taken all the pressure and all these problems on myself, and of course I've shared all the successes."

Although Anna hopes for the day that Brady will have more time to be home, and with the family, she realizes it may never come.

"I don't think he'll never retire, and I probably won't either. I'll be there trying to work as long as I can. I love my husband, I am proud to be his wife, to be a part of his dreams, the dreams that we have shared, and have made reality by first putting God in front of us ... If I had to do it all over again. I would do it exactly the same ... with Brady."

Mother-in-Law, Cecile Bell, was truly a strong woman for me during the initial years of my company.

The original "Brady Bunch," son Brady III, Brady Jr., Father Brady Sr., and son Brady Tyrone.

Chapter 11

My Father

Regardless of all the things Brady may have missed out on in life, as a result of not having a father, he says he does not harbor any resentment, or ill feeling towards his father.

"Someone once asked me did I hate my father for leaving the family when I was just a baby, and do I respect him today, as my father?

First of all, I don't hate anyone, I certainly cannot hate my own father. It is true, he did leave us. Yes, mama did have to work very, very, hard, sometimes working two jobs as a maid doing whatever she could to support us. To hate someone is a concentrated effort. It consumes a tremendous amount of energy, to physically hate a person costs too much. I can't afford the price.

As for resentment, you have to go back to my loving environment from my childhood. What could've been better. What was there for me to resent. He wasn't around, what did I miss. You don't miss something you never had.

The Lord loves me in spite of all my sins, so who am I ... what right have I to hate! How can I disdain my own father?

I don't mind telling the world that I love my father!"

"I regret what I did ... I'm sorry! Sorry! Sorry! For the rest of my life I'm sorry. Another wife, another lifetime ... I learned the truth too late.

It was all a tragic waste of time on my part. Lord, I loved A.C. I even married her, but the arrogance of my youth could never allow me to forgive her. Forgive her for what I thought she'd done to me. So we never lived together in the same house as man and wife. There was one thing about A.C., she was my first lady, my first love, and never did she try to poison my son's mind against me.

It doesn't seem real to me now, it's almost like a dream that happened long ago. I was 17 years old. I was a good student, not only academically, but athletically as well. Although my son is credited for his outstanding athletic abilities, I was in fact, a much better athlete back in my day. You see, in the 1930's a Black man in sports was unheard of in Austin, Texas. I never got the opportunity to become great! I guess I was born too soon.

I remember the day that it happened because I had a large hole in the seat of my already patched overalls. The kids at school gave me the devil. It was summer time, hot and sticky, pitch black with nothing but the faint light of the moon and stars to light your way. There were no fancy street lamps or porch lights on the poor side of town.

Two burly, red-faced, white men materialized from the car, duded-up in cowboy boots with spurs that clinged and clanged as they walked. They were topped off with fancy wide brimmed Stetson hats, and their weighty belts sagged from their waists.

"Boy, are you Brady Keys?" one of the rangers asked. "Yes sir." "Do you know A.C. Hutchinson?"

"Yes sir!" "Did you big (impregnate) her?" He hesitated with his response.

"Boy, I said did you big her?" "Yes sir, I ... I ... did." "Are you going to marry her?" "Yes sir. A.C., her mother, and my mother have everything all arranged. As soon as I graduate from high school, we will get married, we all agreed."

The two men looked at each other and smiled. One of the rangers tipped back his hat, and spat in the direction of where Brady, Sr., was standing, and said, "Well that's not what her father said. I'm sorry boy, I'm gonna have to take you in! A.C.'s father has filed a formal complaint against you."

Brady, Sr., was terrified. As he began to think of the harsh realities of jail, his knees began to shake and he began to sweat. He also remembered the hole in the seat of his pants, which seemed to grow even bigger.

Brady, Sr., attempted to defend himself, "Her father? Her father has nothing to do with this! He doesn't even know me. He doesn't even live at home with A.C. I don't understand what is going on here."

"Well, I'm sure sorry about this boy, I'm still gonna have to run you in," the Ranger replied.

The night he spent in jail seemed to him like the longest night of his life. The Rangers did attempt to protect him by isolating him in an empty cell that was equipped to house 20 beds.

Brady, Sr., vividly recalled every aspect of that night. The jail reeked of vomit, urine, stale liquor and the musty stench of hardened criminals.

From a nearby cell, he heard someone say. "Hey boy, what you in here for?" "I don't know," Brady, Sr., replied. "You shouldn't be in THAT cell boy. Two men just got KILLED in there, get out of there boy!" he warned.

Afraid of what he had just heard, young Brady, Sr., moved back nervously against the cell wall.

At that time, he heard the sound of another vaguely familiar voice from that same cell.

48

"Brady Keys, is that you?" Brady, Sr., removed himself from the wall as he recognized the familiar voice. It was Conley. He had gone to school with Conley's younger brother. Conley was in jail for killing a white man on the main street of town in broad daylight.

"Yes, yes, it's Brady. Conley?" "Brady, you listen to me. Don't you listen to them, they put you over there for your protection so that you wouldn't have to be over here with us."

Conley then snatched the man from his feet, flung him into the wall, and yelled, "If you tell that boy anything like that again, you'll have to deal with ME!"

Brady felt a bit more at ease. But throughout the night, he was tortured with the echoing sounds of sharp screams, dirty laughter, and the constant clamoring of keys.

The following day, Brady, Sr., was escorted from his jail cell to the judge. He wore the same worn-out overalls with a hole in his seat. After the restless night he'd spent in jail, he felt removed from the event that was about to take place … his wedding.

With A.C. and her mother to his right side, and his mother and brother to his left, Brady, Sr., faced the judge who was to marry him. The man who had supposedly concocted the entire incident, A.C.'s father, wasn't even present.

"Are you going to marry this girl," the judge snapped. "Yes sir. It has already been arranged by our parents, just as soon as I graduate from school, we … we …" "I mean NOW! RIGHT NOW! Boy are you going to marry her NOW!"

"Sir, I will marry a snake right now if it will get me out of here," Brady responded.

Although he went ahead with the marriage ceremony, Brady, Sr., felt betrayed by A.C., and her family. As a result, he not only refused to ride home in the same car with his new bride, but he also refused to have anything else to do with her.

On May 19, 1937 Brady Keys, Jr., was born. By the time of young Brady's birth, the situation between his mother and father was not any better. Brady, Sr., had no money, and no job prospects. Consequently, he left Austin and moved to San Antonio to seek employment.

After a few years, he eventually left San Antonio for San Francisco where he fell in love with another woman, who he decided to marry. He asked A.C. for a divorce, she consented, and they were both able to move forward with their lives.

Before they moved forward with their lives, they were able to have some closure for the two of them. A.C. explained to Brady, Sr., the mysterious circumstances behind their shot gun wedding, which at the time was also a mystery to both her, and her mother.

It was with this revelation that Brady, Sr., became regretful for the things he had done, as a result of feeling forced into marriage.

Brady Keys, Sr., died on April 8, 1993. The last interaction between the two before his demise was one that Brady, Jr., will never forget. "My father committed suicide. He became a hermit-like person. He called me once and said he had cancer, he thought he had cancer, and he said "I need your help". I did what I always do when someone says they need help, I do it with the same vigor I do everything else. I called and got an appointment for him. They didn't give appointments, but I got him an appointment within two weeks. I took care of everything.

My father had not accepted Jesus Christ, so I called my daughter Yvette, and she had him accept Jesus Christ. That night when my father was making his transformation, he was getting ready to come and stay with me, but that night Satan moved in on him.

Brady described the last interaction he had with his father as satanic and almost like an exorcism. "The night before my father died, my sister, Jackie, called me and said she wanted me to talk to my father. I said okay. We got on the phone and we started talking and it was a conversation like no other. I stopped in the middle of the conversation and said, "Brady Keys this is not you I'm talking to. So help me God, I said" this is Satan, you are possessed now," and he said "yes." I told him Yvette is going to call you and you are going to accept Jesus Christ and you're going to be saved. He said, "it's too late, it's too late, it's too late," … in a different voice, and I said Jackie we are not talking to our father.

He hung up and that's when I called Yvette. She worked with him, and he accepted Jesus Christ. The next morning about 5:00,

Yvette and her husband woke up at the same time and said "he's dead, Satan has attacked him." She called me. All during that time, the lady next door said she had heard something beating him up, beating his head up against the wall, something was just throwing him around. My father was possessed. He got the shotgun, put it in his mouth, and blew his brains out. That is not a Keys thing as I know of, and God be my witness, since that day I can spot the devil. It's a tone you never forget, it's clearly different as anything, it's not even a living thing."

Sister Jackie and her family, back row l-r, Timothy, Jackie, and Tracy, Jr. Front row, l-r, Nicole, Tracy, Sr., and Kristopher.

Chapter 12

Fatherhood

"My relationship with my children is very special. We are just like any other average black American family, however, in many ways we are very different."

Brady recalled when he first became a father.

"When I was in high school, I had a very brief intimate relationship with a young lady named Barbara Thomas. About a month later I received a phone call from her informing me that she was pregnant. I was young, wild, and crazy. I was just out enjoying my fool self, having a good time. I couldn't even imagine me getting a girl pregnant, so I simply dispelled it from my immature mind.

Some months later her mother phoned. She wanted my mother and me to come to the house. I asked why? She then told me ... to see my children. I then realized something had actually happened. When I arrived at her mother's house, I saw these twin baby girls, named Lynn and Linda Thomas, sleeping in a crib, that's when they told me the babies were mine.

I remember looking down at the two little babies saying, who's are they? "Brady, they are YOUR kids! You made them, you and Barbara," her mother said.

I began to die inside. I was standing there looking down at those two little bundles of life, and my mind refused to accept them as my own. I couldn't fathom myself at sixteen a daddy! My dreams slowly began to wither, and die at the roots. At that moment her mother looked me square in the eyes, and unwaveringly told me, "We're not asking anything from you. You don't have to worry about them, because you will never see them again!"

She was right, I never saw both twins alive again. I heard Linda died later. So they were right after all, I was never to see my twins again.

Life continued, I was allowed to graduate from high school, and pursue my career as a professional football player, undisturbed, so it seemed to the world. Some eight years later, in a Los Angeles supermarket, there she was ... Barbara Thomas!

I walked over to her, and asked her if I could see my daughter. Her curtness made it clear, the years had not softened her towards me. She agreed to let me see Lynn, BUT I couldn't mention to her that I was her father. At this point she had three more children, and I was told to pick out which one was my daughter.

I agreed to her conditions, she then warned me that this would be the absolute last time I laid eyes on Lynn. It was easy to spot Lynn, she looked more like me than the other children. Yes, some twenty years would pass before I would see my little girl again.

Brady Bunch at Jamie Keys' graduation from Darton College in 1995.

Chapter 13

Lynn

"I always had a haunting suspicion I was more than just different from the rest of my siblings. Not just because I looked so different, you could say I was the black sheep of the family. I often wondered why mama would get so upset with me more so than the other kids. Now I know ... it was the pain that ached in her heart. I reminded her so much of the father that I never knew ... my father that she secretly scorned!

I remember the day it all happened. It was a day that would change my life. It was a cold day in February, 1976. Uncle Gordon's (Poochy) wife passed away. I went down to Cleveland, Ohio to represent the family.

When I went to view the body everyone commented on how so much like my father I looked. I heard this over, and over again. Little did I know that they meant my natural father ... Brady Keys, Jr.

Well, after everyone had left the house, Uncle Poochy and I were alone. I was sitting down, thumbing lazily through a picture album strolling down memory lane. My eyes came to rest on a picture of me, my sister Cherly, and my daddy.

I said to Poochy, 'Look at this old picture of daddy and us.' Uncle Poochy stared at me for a moment. He pulled this red book from the drawer and said, 'that's not your daddy! This is your daddy! Brady Keys, Jr., he is your FATHER!'

He pointed at the young black man on the cover with his fingers trembling, I looked at him and laughing said, I don't look like HIM! I stood there looking at my Uncle Poochy, poor man must be going into shock, after loosing his wife, I thought.

'This is your FATHER!' he demanded. When I looked at Uncle Poochy again, this time something in his eyes told me he wasn't loosing his mind, or suffering from grief, mental fatigue, or any of those things. Suddenly, I wasn't laughing anymore. I took the book. The next day I asked my grandmother was this Brady Keys my father? Her face turned slate gray, as she grimaced, then walked away. Around every corner in my mind, Brady Keys' name mimicked. I couldn't get home fast enough to confront the only person that could put this awful hoax to rest.

When I arrived home I looked at my mother, she knew something was amiss. Perhaps grandmama had phoned ahead to warn her. I didn't know and didn't care. Mama, I said, IS BRADY KEYS MY FATHER!

It seemed like an eternity before she answered me. 'Yes', mama finally replied. 'Yes!' My God! My heart sunk down to my feet! Why didn't she tell me? When was she going to tell me? How could she have kept something like this from me! I had the right to know!!

My mother told me how I came to be, and about my infamous father. He was a buddy of Uncle Poochy. One day when her parents weren't home Brady came by. Well, one thing led to another, things got totally out of control. She was only a mere child of sixteen, she didn't know anything about sex.

He forced himself on her ... nine months later my sister Linda, and I were born. She also told me that Brady's mother didn't want anything ... NOTHING to stand in her son's way. He was going to become a professional football player. As she spoke, it seemed like my mind went into a dream. This just wasn't happening to me! Things like this only happened in the movies.

I felt numb inside, but one thing was for damn sure ... I was going to Pittsburgh to meet this man face to face, eyeball to eyeball for some answers.

When we arrived in Pittsburgh my stomach was in knots. When we reached the Keys Estate, I was shaking so badly I could hardly stand.

There he was, I would know him anywhere ... because I looked just like him. He came to the car, opened the door and took my hand. I introduced him to my ex-husband, my daughter Nakia, she was only eight months, and my son, Kenneth. He

56

ushered us into the house. He and I went into a huge room filled with trophies. Brady held my hand. My palms were sweaty, his were warm and dry. The power in his grip told me to allay my fears ... I was home.

He sat in a big leather chair looking at me. He asked me so many questions about Uncle Poochy, and my mother. To his surprise, they had told me next to nothing. We spent hours talking. Funny it seemed like I knew him all my life. He didn't tell anyone in the family about me, including his pretty wife Anna.

Anna's reception was unbelievably warm. Later I found out she wasn't told about me until later the next day. The rest of my new family was just curious. I always wondered where I got my strong drive from ... now I know.

I hold no remorse toward my mother, nor my father Brady for not telling me who I was sooner. But I do encourage other parents to not hide things from your children because you never know when those secrets will come back to haunt you."

Lynn, (right above), with her daughter Nakia is still beautiful in spite of being a grandmother (from son Kenny) which makes me a great-grandfather.

Brady Tyrone, Yvette, Brady Jr., Jamie, Brady III, & Rodney at one of their monthly dinner meetings.

Chapter 14

The Boys

"When I saw little Tyrone, I guess I'd have to say it was heaven – a man having his first son. I was only about 18 or 19 years old. I was very proud of Tyrone, but he was very sick. I would literally die for that child, and all of my children. I remember when Tyrone was sick, he had asthma when he was a child. He couldn't breathe, and we had no money, so we couldn't buy any medicine. Tyrone was literally fading away and turning blue because he was just so clogged up, and he was too little to breathe out of his mouth, so you know what I did – I sucked all the mucous out of his nose. I can't believe I did that, but my boy lived! —Brady Keys, Jr.

Tyrone

"I was 15 years old when I came to live with my father in Pittsburgh. I really never got to know my father. Only now am I beginning to understand, through myself. You see, my father and

I are so much alike that you have to step away to look up close. You see, I came along from the outside, a son from a previous marriage. I knew of my father, but I never KNEW him, there is a distinct difference between the two!

It was the strong love of my mother that sustained me. I am very close with my mother. She is my foundation. She was not only my mother, but my father as well. I love my mother, everyday of my life.

I remember the feeling when I first came to live with daddy. There was Buzzy, Rodney, and Jamie, then me. It was like I wore an invisible shield. It was like, you're on your own kid. Make it the best way you can!

I felt cheated. The other boys were born into the comfortable two parent household. They had everything, where I didn't. I knew what it was like to struggle. They never really experienced real pain. So there I was, on the outside looking in for the most part. Daddy was always going and coming, for as long as I can remember. The time that he did spend with us we cherished. There just wasn't any time to get to know him personally. Today, I see things differently. I see myself wanting to get to know my father better. I want to learn the business from the inside out like he does. My father expects so much from me. It's hard trying to please him. I think I spend more time trying to please him, than I do myself. It's like you're on this big stage, everybody has their eyes glued on YOU!

These last few years have really opened my eyes. I have learned so much about the business, so much about myself, and which direction I want to go. I feel at this stage of my life that I am confident I can run the business successfully, if necessary.

Buzzy

He was born in Colorado and when he was born he and Anna both had jaundice. The doctors came to me and asked me which one did I want them to save because they would have to let one of them die. This was in Colorado, and there were only about 6 blacks in the city, and Buzzy was very light skinned. When I went to see him they wouldn't let me in the hospital because there were not any black babies. My wife was very, very fair skinned because she is half white, and they wouldn't let me in the hospital because there were not any black babies there. When they found out they were sick, and they had to page me because my wife was too sick to make any decisions for herself, so they asked me which one did I want to live and which one to die. This was their first experience with a Brady Keys, I said, "You are not going to let none of my people die, they are both going to live. I am not going to make a stupid decision like that to give you an out. Both of them are going to live and that is my decision. Two live!" If I had made the decision to accept one or the other they would've let the other one die, I said no way, no way in hell! —Brady Keys, Jr.

"I am glad that I was born into this family. It is true that we have a lot to be thankful for. My father always made us work very very hard for everything. That way he was sure that we appreciated whatever we got. It's not easy working for my family. My father demands that you give your "all" to the business, and you put forth your all in whatever you do! So, that is why I must do my very best! Not only to try and please dad, but to please myself."

Rodney

*He was 4 1/2 months premature, and it was very traumatic because my ex-wife, Delores, had hit me up for all my money while I was playing football. She took me to court and tied up everything I had in court. It was a **horrible** time ... luckily I had some insurance, a few insurance cards I was able to cash in a policy and get the doctors started on him. They had to start the operation on him to correct all the things they needed to correct. He had about five operations on his eyes, he had corrective shoes, corrective this, corrective that, and that's why I call him my bionic son.*

The first deal I closed for Burger King, this huge deal, I made the lawyer I hired work with Rodney to teach him how to do it. So Rodney was the lead lawyer, and I made the lawyer work for Rodney. He's very experienced based on me giving him all these lead shots, so he has the most knowledge at this point. —Brady Keys, Jr.

"I am proud to be a Keys. It is an honor. I am proud to have two such fine parents that I love so very much. If it had not been for the strong influence of my parents, I wouldn't be where I am today. My father made something out of nothing. I want so very much to bring something into the family business. I want to prove first, to myself that I have the ability to be a successful lawyer, and businessman. If my dad can make a million dollars out of nothing, I should be able to make 10 million out of what both my parents have done for me.

Although my father never got a degree from college he instilled in me how very important it was to obtain a formal education. I know that education is the key, one of the main elements of success. I try and talk to the young brothers at different high schools and tell them that it is going to take a lot more than a high school education to make it in today's world. I heard these kids talk, and I can't believe my ears! Some of them think, well after high school, that's it!

Hello world, boy are they in for a very rude awakening. As parents, I think we can't school our children enough about the importance of higher education."

A fond memory I have was my dad taking us to Bull Moose Lodge in Canada, in Lake of the Woods Ontario. Despite all the business things he was doing, he would fly us up there. We'd go fishing, hiking, and hunting, go back to nature, and we'd do it as a family.

We survived scares by a real life bear that would come and scratch on our cabin. We took Len Burnett's kids one year, and we listened to Michael Jackson's "Going Back to Indiana" play over and over and over.

When I think back about that, that was a very fond memory with the family.

Jamie

Jamie was always sick. He had eczema and we didn't know it. It was horrible when we found out about it; for a year and a half he cried everyday. He was miserable because we didn't know he had eczema. He was always sick, and he had no hair. When we figured it out, Anna took care of that. She literally nourished that boys scalp. She did this everyday, she just sat there and nourished the poor child. She actually fertilized his skull and caused that hair to grow by herself. The doctor even said it was not possible.

Jamie is the youngest, he's grown up through all of this when I was traveling all over the world, and doing a lot of things. It's just an act of God that he has not strayed, because I was traveling all the time. It's different having a daddy that was a professional football player, and an All-Pro football player, and having done all these "first" things. Jamie had the least of me, that's why when I get things from my memorabilia I always give it to Jamie and not the rest of them. —Brady Keys, Jr.

One memory that always stands out, and the one I always think about is the first commercial me and my father did together. I was eight years old, and late one night after we finished rehearsal for The Little Miss Detroit Pageant, for which I was an escort, my father decided to make a commercial for the new special they had at the chicken stores. It was called the "Wing Thing Special", which was five wings for a dollar. I was dressed up in this white chicken outfit, standing next to my father flapping my arms like a chicken as he talked. When he finished talking, he turned to me and said, "And this is my little chicken." That's when I took off the head of the chicken outfit and stood next to my father, and turned to the camera and smiled.

That commercial played all over Detroit, and I became known everywhere as my dad's "little chicken." When I went to school everybody knew me from the commercial, which made it that much more special because I guess not too many eight year olds get to make a commercial with their father, not to mention having it played all over the city, and then everybody, all your friends, knowing you for that commercial."

Today, Brady has a cherished, close relationship with his children, but he does admit that he has some regrets about his relationship with his kids, and their perception of him.

"They have this image of this father that's a great businessman. It really impedes them because they can't see me for what I am, and they don't know what to see me as. Am I the father, am I the football player father, am I the businessman, what am I? So, they are really meek and humble, which makes it easy to keep them out of trouble."

Although he does view his ability to influence their behavior as a blessing, he does have a preference of how he would like his children to view him.

"I would like for them to see me as a father-businessman, but they get it all mixed up because there is a football image, a hero image, the father image, the businessman image. It's really hard for them."

Brady recalled a period of adversity for the family, which the kids could not comprehend because of their perception of him.

"I remember one time when I was in the coal business. I had a bad time, one of my real bad times, and I called a family meeting. I told the family that I was broke. We were living in a home that was over one hundred thousand dollars, but I told them it was just really hard times. I remember they looked at me, and they didn't see that. They couldn't see me having problems. Whatever it was, they could only see me solving the problem."

Chapter 15

Yvette

It was Yvette who reopened my eyes to Christ! She is such a dedicated soul unto the Lord. I have learned so much about myself through the Lord, and it was my daughter that so unselfishly let her inner light shine on me, and I just thank God I wasn't too blind to see it. —Brady Keys, Jr.

"My dad, Brady Keys, Jr, is one of the most unique human beings God has created. And to well, appreciate the quality, the talent, and energetic force God has planted in him, you need to have a spiritual mind set.

As a teenager I had developed great anger against my dad. But through the grace of God, and mercy of a loving God, I learned what true love is, and how forgiveness leads to a life that is full of blessings. My dad is an awesome blessing to me. He's like a strong oak tree planted by God to disperse fruits. He has something to impart in everyone who comes in contact with him.

King David in the Bible was a great man, chosen by God to be a great King. With all his sin and pride he still was a man after God's heart, and God said in Psalms 89:19 that "He laid help upon one that is mighty and has exalted one chosen out of the people." Verse 20 says, "I have found David my servant; with my holy oil have I anointed him." I believe my dad is as David appointed and anointed to accomplish many things, and to point many to the Lord.

God gave me the honor of leading my dad in the prayer of salvation. On many occasions I experience the spirit of the Lord impressing me to give my dad a word or spiritual insight, and at the same token God has used my dad in awesome ways with his wisdom to let me see natural things bring out spiritual principles.

I especially learned this in the five years of being a radio announcer on WJIZ when my dad was owner, and sitting in the Monday morning meeting he would hold. Those five years were a great time and opportunity for me being under such a great leader as my dad. God gives him great insight and faith, and it's an awesome wonder to see the things God uses him to do. God has allowed me to explore my gifts of talent in many ways, thanks to my dad. Doors have opened for me to do things that to this day still amaze me. I thank God that he looked so far in time to create Brady Keys, Jr, and to let me be blessed to have him as my dad.

Jim Brown crashes into Brady causing a life threatening blood vessel injury that cost the Steeler's a championship.

ક ક ક ક ક ક ક

Part 3

Taking It To
The Next Level

ક ક ક ક ક ક ક

FROM **FOOTBALL** to **FINANCE**

Brady as a young Pittsburgh Steeler and young businessman — *From Football to Finance,* **the picture that inspired the first book on Brady's life.**

Chapter 16

Football to Finance

In 1966, another one of Brady's childhood dreams came true. He was selected All-Pro Defensive Back as a member of the Pittsburgh Steelers, and started in the 1967 Pro Bowl.

That year the Pro Bowl was held at the Los Angeles Coliseum. As their names were called over the loudspeaker, each starter entered the field to the drum rolls and thunderous roar of the crowd. Brady anxiously awaited the calling of his name ... "Brady Keys, Pittsburgh Steelers, right cornerback!"

As he heard his name called, Brady flung his head in the air and sprinted into the crowd's view. At that moment the only thing that mattered to him was playing the game he had always dreamed of playing, and to impress his wife Anna, sons Tyrone, Buzzy and Rodney, daughter Yvette, his mother A.C., and other relatives and friends. All of who were in the stands eagerly awaiting the appearance of their hero.

At the day's end, Brady and the other players from the East were the victors. After the game, Brady stood on the field alone ruminating over the events of that day. He had played the game with the creme de la creme. Players like Dave Parks, John Unitas, and Gayle Sayers.

He had played well both defensively and offensively. He was making a lot of money, his home life was happy, at this point Brady felt he had climaxed in his career. He now wondered what his next challenge would be.

After the game, Brady went home to partake in a family feast. There was a smorgasbord of food prepared, and his entire family was present. Along with his six year old, Brady Keys III (Buzzy), and two year old Rodney, Brady's mother and stepfather, and mother in law were in attendance.

Brady looked around the table and reflected for a moment on how far he had come. It seemed not so long ago he had watched his mother serve him bread and syrup with sweetwater for dinner. Now he sat at a dinner table with his family in a mansion that was fit for royalty. It was truly a dream come true for him, and he realized it was time for him to move on, and enter the next phase of his life.

Brady, who was 29 at that time, felt he had about six good seasons left in football. He figured he could earn about another $250,000 before throwing in the towel.

Brady announced to his family, "Well folks, I'm afraid my football days are about over." After he gained his families undivided attention, he continued, "By the power of God, I've been blessed to achieve every goal that I set for myself, and my family. I've been proven among the best, so now an end of an era swiftly approaches, and it's time to move on to bigger and better things."

His mother-in-law asked, "You mean you have something in mind that will pay as well as football, something you can keep on doing after you're thirty six, right?"

"Cecile, you're dead right," Brady responded. "I'm going into business. How do you like the chicken? It's delicious, I know it is. That deep home fried crispy taste is no accident. That, my family, is the result of weeks of experimenting with A.C, Anna, Cecile, and myself to come up with an absolutely lip smacking batter. We have so much confidence in our secret recipe that I plan to open the first Brady Keys' All-Pro Chicken store in San Diego two weeks from today.!"

None of his family challenged his idea. He felt this would be the ideal plan to make the transition from football to business. Although it may have appeared to be a spontaneous decision, Brady's family knew him well enough to know he wouldn't enter any type venture unprepared. And there were several people present who were aware of his announcement and desire at age eight to become a football player and a business man.

At the end of the 1966 football season, Brady returned to Los Angeles to work in one of his friend's restaurants. He didn't work for pay, instead he worked for experience. He was unable to obtain money from the banks, so he borrowed it from the Steelers. With his first store he did the contracting and the design himself.

On Friday, January 27, 1967, at 4:30 pm, Brady Keys, Jr., opened his first store at 5067 Logan Street in San Diego. The first day response was encouraging, All-Pro Fried Chicken grossed $65. Even on that first day, Brady had a plan. "All I need are 200 All-Pro Fried Chicken Franchises. I'm going to become the first Black franchisor in corporate history," he stated.

Soon after his initial store opening, he opened a second store in San Diego. However, it was not a success. Brady carefully analyzed the situation, and he realized his mistake was not studying the dining out practices of white suburbia. He also later realized that the site for the store was also wrong. He needed a better marketing strategy, and more money.

After several unsuccessful attempts to obtain the necessary funds, Brady decided to approach the owners of the Steelers, the Rooney family, for the money. However, he was uncertain as to how willing they would be to take the risk in investing in him.

First week with Anna M. Keys and her cousin Anthony Benna who was the second employee hired.

"The Beginning" Brady Keys' First Store.

Chapter 22

Move to the Motor City

Brady decided to expand his dream. In 1970, he arrived in Detroit with a plan to promote black entrepreneurship in franchising. During this time, franchising had received negative publicity, but Brady stood firm behind his belief.

He saw how franchising could benefit not only blacks, but the economy as well. Dedicated to his plight, Brady spoke to a U.S. Senate sub-committee on the subject of franchising. Specifically, he addressed his concerns about the relationship between the White retailers and the Black community.

Brady believed White merchants were failing the Black community. He felt Black entrepreneurs could fulfill the needs of the Black community that White merchants and retailers had neglected. In their abandonment of Blacks, Brady felt that consequently they were being left without necessary resources.

He also addressed the need for a middle-class that included both Black and White merchants and businessmen in the innercity. Unfortunately, the majority of Blacks left in the Black community did not possess the skills, or the finances to undertake such a major project.

Brady called on foundations and corporations to provide the financial support for this venture. He needed money for special training programs, and for the existing businesses that lacked funds. He firmly believed he'd become a successful entrepreneur, and his primary objective was to, "create a working organism of people both Black and White in America."

As a result of his relentless efforts, Brady was appointed by President Richard Nixon to the National Advisory Council for Minority Business Enterprises, and to the President's Council of Equal Opportunity Community for the International Franchise

Association. He became the first Black man to serve as a board member of that association.

While on a trip to Washington, D.C., Brady was leaving a Minority Business meeting when he accidentally backed into the founder of Burger King, Mr. James. W. McLamore.

McLamore had heard all about Brady, and he feared Brady was headed for troubles with his business because he was receiving money from too many different sources.

After their initial encounter, they met several times thereafter. Although McLamore wasn't impressed with Brady's style of business, he was impressed with Brady, and he made him an offer he couldn't dare refuse. McLamore owned a store in the inner city of Detroit that wasn't making any money. He told Brady that if he could make the store turn a profit within 6 months then he could have it for little to nothing.

Within five months, Brady and his staff went from $25,000 in sales per month, to $65,000 a month in sales. It became the number one Burger King in the nation.

As a result of the success of this East side store, Brady was able to obtain three more stores. His stores did so well, he began to travel across the country as a good will ambassador for franchising. However, his success did have its downfalls.

Because he was the lone Black pioneer for franchising, and way ahead of his time, many people, both Blacks and Whites, were skeptical of him and his success.

During the time of Brady's successes with franchising times were difficult for him because he had nobody to turn to for advice. He was the first of his kind. He was solely responsible for setting the course for future generations of Black franchisors.

Since many people did not know how to take Brady, the rumors began to circulate throughout Detroit. It had been rumored that Brady Keys was a front for the White establishment. His Black employees became suspicious of his "sudden" ownership of four Burger King stores in Detroit.

Brady's rare appearances in his stores only added fuel to the fire. His employees suspected he was indeed perpetrating a fraud. The rumors traveled fast. Eventually, Fred Patman, a lawyer, caught wind of the rumor mill.

After hearing the rumors, Patman contacted Kenneth Cockrel, who was also a lawyer. Cockrel was particularly interested in issues concerning Black entrepreneurship. The Keys Group employees became more weary and began to make demands of their phantom boss.

They demanded a tangible Black owner. It was also rumored that Patman had motives for getting involved with this case. It was said that he desired ownership of Brady's stores.

The news media fed into the rumors, and they fanned the flames regarding heresay about Brady and his alleged role as a front for White people. Needless to say, the negative publicity was detrimental to Brady's reputation. As far as his employees were concerned, the media attention validated their suspicions.

The tension among the ranks of Burger King began to mount, and Fred Patman was there to take full advantage of the situation. He instigated the one thing Burger King, and its financial investors feared the most, a strike.

Brady had appointed his childhood friend, Reggie Smith, to manage all his business affairs during his absence. The two had previously worked together in the Pittsburgh office. Smith moved to Detroit to become manager of Brady's Burger King franchises. He was also instrumental in helping develop the concept of "Have it Your Way", which is now the trademark phrase for Burger King nationally.

Burger King's fear eventually became a reality, their employees walked off the job, which brought operations to a halt. The investors were nervous about the strike and considered pulling out of the corporation. Also on the day of the strike, a monopolistic suit was filed against Brady and Metropolitan life, a financial investor in Brady's stores, who was named as an accessory.

During the strike, several members of the management team received death threats. After the threats began, an anonymous tip was reported that one of Brady's Burger King restaurants would be riddled with shotgun blasts if certain demands were not met.

This alarmed many members of management, especially Reggie Smith, who vanished without warning.

Brady felt enough was enough. He appointed Jim Reese to assume Smith's position, and he related the incident to his Chief of Operations in New York, Al Talley. He recommended that Talley come to Detroit to evaluate the situation, not only because of the strike, but also because there was a substantial amount of money missing from his stores. After several days had passed, there was still no information on the whereabouts of Smith.

Upon his arrival to Detroit, Talley received open hostility from all sides. He had been asked to come down for a few days, but he ended up staying several months.

Over 100 of the striking employees called a meeting without their lawyer present. They wanted to discuss their strategy for a massive rally they'd planned, and most importantly they wanted to destroy Brady, and the businesses he'd worked so hard to build.

Brady and his management team received word from Doug Bobo, a former strike lawyer for the company, as to what the striking employees had planned. As the executives attempted to come up with a solution to their problem, Brady stood up abruptly and proceeded to make a mad dash for the door.

"Mr. Keys, what in the hell are you doing? What's going on," Doug asked.

On his way out the door, Brady responded, "I'm going to the meeting, ALONE, and tell them exactly what's on my mind, and DAMNIT THEY ARE GOING TO LISTEN!"

Doug stood up and said, "No, Mr. Keys. You can't go there by yourself man, that's crazy!"

Doug grabbed his sawed off shotgun from the table and went after Brady. At the same time, the other employees followed with their weapons in hand in an effort to support their fearless leader.

Brady stopped them, "No, I'm the person that they are angry with. I am the person they want to see. They are asking for me, Brady Keys, Jr.!! I am the person who is either going to make or break the deal. That is my restaurant damnit! Mine! Ain't nobody gonna keep me away from my own store! If they want to address some issues, they will address them to me, and me ALONE!"

As Brady made his way to his restaurant to confront his disgruntled employees, they were plotting their scheme to bring him down. They were dumfounded by his presence when Brady entered the room alone.

At the top of his voice he shouted, "I am the real Brady Keys!! I am the owner of the Keys Group Burger King stores. I am a Black businessman, just like you are a Black employee! I created this company for people like you, so that you can have the opportunity to experience what happens in the real world of business. NOBODY owns me! No White folks own me! I am Brady Keys. Look, if you want to address some issues, address them to me, Brady Keys! Now I admit that I have not been coming up here to be with you. I admit that I have been busy doing other things. What I have been doing is campaigning in your behalf. I have been talking to the people in Washington, testifying before the Senate, to make damn sure that other Blacks like yourselves might have the opportunity to go into franchising. I am the only Black man in franchising thus far. There is room for many more Black people to venture into franchising. I want to share my knowledge with the world! I admit that I have been remiss in not sharing myself with you, THAT AIN'T GONNA CHANGE! Don't look for me to be here holding your hand, look for me to be your leader. But look for me to be a leader for others as well!"

"Now, we can compromise, if you want to. But you WILL NOT force me into doing anything! You WILL NOT force me into closing my stores down, you cannot do that! The WORLD could not! So what the hell makes you any different from the world! You must sit down and look at the issues, because if you put me out of business, you put an entire generation of people out of business! So you gain what? And you lose what? As Black people, you lose everything! EVERYTHING!"

The employees were astonished as they sat and listened. They told him they desired a union. He responded, "We can talk about a union or anything else, AFTER you go back to work!"

101

By now Brady knew he had accomplished his mission, and if he played his cards right, the strike would end. He suggested they have a "coming together" party to completely break the ice. They accepted the offer.

That was the end of round one, they still had to go to court. Fred Patman scheduled a court hearing to obtain a union contract for the employees. Still, the employees remained oblivious to Patman's true motives. Everyone knew that Brady's Burger King stores had lost a lot of money as a result of the strike, and Patman saw this as an opportunity to seize ownership of the company.

Patman tried to obtain an order from the court to shut down Brady's businesses permanently. In turn, this would allow him to manipulate the corporation into selling the stores to him.

After deliberating for several days, the court returned a verdict in Brady's favor. After being shut down for nearly seventeen days, the stores were immediately put back into operation. In the end everyone won because the court also ruled in favor of the union contract for the employees.

The strike really affected Burger King. The corporation was strong armed into hiring Fred Patman's cousin, Claude Patman as Vice President of Burger King Corporation. Also, Bob Williams, who Patman represented in the monopoly suit, seized an opportunity to purchase a Burger King franchise. This deal eliminated the perceived monopoly Brady had on the market.

However, Claude Patman's position was short lived. Burger King realized he had a negative impact on their business, so they relieved him of his duties.

In contrast, Bob Williams' stores were very profitable. Al Talley got the company out of financial trouble, and Reggie Smith was eventually found to be alive and well, but he never returned to work for Brady. When he did resurface he acquired his own Burger King Store.

Walt & Reggie were the first of many to turn on Brady but he never stopped loving them even unto this day.

1st Burger King in Detroit history owned by a black man.

Chapter 23

If You Build Your Community, You Build Your Business

Even though he had the Burger King, and KFC stores, Brady knew that it would take more to get his Keys Group Company to the next level. With Brady everything is about going to the next level, because he never settles for, or accepts the status quo.

The first thing he set out to do was to get his employees to distinguish between Burger King and Keys Group, because they were not one in the same. Brady needed to gain the trust of his employees, and gain their loyalty.

After the strikes were resolved and business was up and running, Brady knew he needed to make some changes within the organization to prevent any further upsets of that magnitude. He knew he needed to gain the loyalty of his employees. He had someone in mind that he knew could be of service to him, his former teammate from his days with the Pittsburgh Steelers, Len Burnett.

Brady enlisted the help of Len even though he knew he had no experience in this particular field of business. After football, Len returned to his educational roots. His major in college had been education so after his tenure with professional football, he began teaching.

However, none of that mattered to Brady because to him Len's lack of expertise and ability in business was not important. He knew they had chemistry.

"I look for people based on chemistry of how we work together, not ability. I can teach ability, or the books can teach ability, but you can't teach chemistry.

And that is the one thing that he and Len had plenty of - chemistry.

Len came to work for the company and at that time his job was to develop personnel policies. Later he became involved in the process of developing the Keys Group Company name.

In order for Brady to make his mark within the community he knew they would have to develop the company name in order for people to know who they were, and that first had to begin with his employees.

It was crucial that the employees began to see Keys Group as a separate entity from Burger King because they had no loyalties to Burger King, which was a major conglomerate without a human face. Brady and Len began to organize campaigns for Keys Group to become involved in the community so they could establish that crucial separate identity.

In order to gain his employees trust and loyalty he knew that he would have to not only make himself available to them, but most importantly he knew he needed to find out how they felt about their jobs and the company, and the only way to do that was to talk to them.

Brady began to meet with his employees, all of them, from the managers to the cooks, the cashiers, and the janitors. He knew that he couldn't tell a cashier how to do his/her job if he didn't know what that job entailed. He also did things to boost the morale of his employees by complimenting and rewarding employees for jobs well done. Most importantly, he rewarded good, hard work with promotions within the company. All Keys Group employees knew that if they worked hard for the company there was plenty of room for upward mobility. People who started out in the company as cashiers and cooks were often promoted to management positions within the restaurant and others were promoted and transferred to the Keys Group offices. Those type efforts were instrumental in gaining the loyalty of his employees, and towards allowing the employees to see Keys Group apart from Burger King.

The next step for Keys Group was to gain the support and trust of the community. In order to do that they became involved in several campaigns, including a lottery loser campaign with the Detroit Lottery, which promoted the image of everybody being a winner. That particular campaign allowed people holding losing lottery tickets to come into Burger King and receive customer discounted or free food items.

The most successful campaign that really catapulted Keys Group was their plight to keep kids off drugs. This campaign led to major publicity for the company which benefitted not only them, but the community as well. Brady's motto was then and still remains today: "Build your community and you build your business."

Keys Group's campaign against drugs was successful and the word spread through the community so much that people with similar plights for kids began to solicit the help of Keys Group. Maxine Willis was one of those solicitors.

"I met Mr. Keys in late 1989. I'd heard of Mr. Keys and all the great things he was doing in the city of Detroit, and his reputation was just outstanding! I was in drug prevention working with children in the community and I met him in an effort to understand what we could do to get more business people involved in drug prevention, and how we could get the community involved. Of course everybody said, you need to talk to Brady Keys, this man is phenomenal. He's doing great things and from a business perspective I just know he will help with a program like this. And sure enough I met Mr. Keys and just like anything he gets involved in, and any advice he gives, you've got to look at how you can take this to the next level.

So, for months we worked together, and I shared with him my idea and dream of having happy, healthy children, and of course that fell right in line with the Keys Group philosophy. From that, one day I said to Mr. Keys, "Your name exemplifies what you are all about. You can take the K-E-Y-S, and Kids Enjoy Yourselves", and it was just in talking that it came up, and that's how we came up with the Keys Kids.

Of course Mr. Keys had the idea as a businessman about television, and using the media. He said to me, "When business people want their product to become a household word they use the media. You're trying to get a message into the home, you have to use the media." My dilemma was that I didn't know enough about the media, but Mr. Keys position was, "you know your vision, and you know your dream. And if you don't know that then you're lost, and there's nothing I can do to help you, and I can't wait for you."

So of course, with his influence he made contacts with some of the stations in the area, and the Keys Kids Television Show gave birth in 1990, and it is still going strong as of 1997."

Detroit Lion Lomas Brown and kids in the company called Kids Enjoy Yourself Without Drugs created by Brady and best friend Maxine Willis.

Norm Haberman, Vice-President of KFC, the Colonel and Brady at KFC Corporation.

Chapter 24

Keys Meets The Colonel

Brady's success with Burger King wasn't enough. He was driven by his burning desire to continue his crusade for blacks in franchising. That desire resulted in him temporarily delegating his responsibilities so he could leave Detroit.

Despite his success with Burger King, he couldn't deny his roots - the chicken business. Brady's All-Pro Chicken Restaurants were doing well, but he wanted more. He began to enlist the help of M.K. Mellot once again. Mellot was in a position to help Brady expand his chicken business. He was a consultant who searched the country for companies with strong merging potential.

Brady's initial attempts at a merger were unsuccessful, and he began to think that his possibilities at a successful merger were limited because of his black business concept. Regardless of his skepticism, he and Mellot continued their quest, and eventually he came up with a possible solution.

"If we're going to be in the chicken business, we should strive to attract the best. And who is the best? Colonel Sanders Kentucky Fried Chicken!"

Brady and Mellot conducted a thorough investigation of KFC. They scrutinized every aspect of the business, and they discovered that KFC and All-Pro were very similar. He also found that KFC was grossing $100 million of business per year.

Pleased with their findings, Brady concocted a well thought out plan to accomplish his merger with KFC. He knew he needed to get to the only person that was capable of making his merger possible. That man was John Y. Brown, the president of KFC. Brown was the man who took the Colonel's idea and globalize it.

Brady wanted to get to Brown, and he was smart enough to know the direct approach would not work. Thanks to his business savvy, he knew any meeting between he and Brown would have to be at the request of Brown. This method would ensure that they would both be on equal ground with a mutual respect for each others business successes.

Brady and Mellot developed a strategy to capture the interest of KFC's lower level executives. The first phase of their plan was successful. However, Brady realized that the the lower level executives had no authority to make the decisions they would require from them.

Mellot then arranged a meeting with Frank King, who was the Vice-President of Acquisitions. Unfortunately, King was no use to them because he suddenly acquired wealth and ended up quitting his job.

Being the impatient man that he was, Brady became frustrated with his inability to get close to Brown. He decided to utilize all of his resources. He called upon an acquaintance he'd encountered through his membership with the International Franchise Association. At one of his meeting with the Senate Sub-Committee, Brady met Senator Harrison Williams (D-NJ) and his Administrative Assistant, Mike Rosenberg. Rosenberg had been very impressed with Brady, so he called on him at this particular time. He told Rosenberg of his desire to meet with Brown. Rosenberg was happy to help Brady, and he proceeded to set up the meeting. Shortly afterwards, Brown requested a meeting with Brady. The meeting was scheduled for May, 13th, six days before Brady's 31st birthday.

Brady caught the 10 a.m. flight to Louisville, Kentucky, and he found a long black limousine with a chauffeur awaiting him at the airport. He felt confident about his impending meeting, but that feeling didn't last very long. Brown was 45 minutes late for their meeting. Brady later found out that Brown had been lunching with one of his good friends from his football days, Paul Hornung.

When they finally met, Brown admitted to Brady that he'd heard some positive things about him. He then said, "Okay Brady, I have an hour, what can I do to help you?"

Brady replied, "I am not seeking help. You asked me here to see you, and I'm ready to listen. I am the president of a company much like yours. A better question to ask would be, what can we do to help each other?"

By the end of their meeting, Brady and Brown had agreed to a tentative joint venture. KFC sent a team to Pittsburgh to thoroughly research and evaluate the foundation of All-Pro Chicken. Incidently, KFC was among many companies that were interested in All-Pro. Some of the companies included Church's, Quaker Oats, the Marriott systems, and the Playboy Clubs, all of whose offers Brady refused.

Four months after their meeting, Brady and Brown became partners. On September 15th, in Washington D.C. at the Hotel Congressional, Brady Keys, Jr., and John Y. Brown announced their historical $2 million merger.

First Black KFC had Brady's picture on it ... Wow!

112

Chapter 25

Albany, Georgia

Owning two major franchises was unheard of, but it was especially unheard of having them both owned by a black man, and in the same city.

Brady owned 11 restaurants, five Burger Kings and six Kentucky Fried Chickens. Needless to say, neither was thrilled with this perceived conflict of interest for Brady. Both franchises feared the possibility of company secrets being passed along to the other.

Inevitably, the day came when Brady was approached about making a choice. KFC told Brady he needed to get out of town, to which his reply was, "make me an offer I can't refuse."

That's exactly what they did. They placed a map of America in front of him and told him to pick where he wanted to go, and if they could do it, they'd do it.

His first choice was Athens, Georgia, but it couldn't be put together. He narrowed his choices down with a couple of very specific qualifiers. "I want to go where it's warm, I want to go where there is a black college that I can help, and black people I can help."

They then suggested Savannah, Georgia, but "I didn't like the community. It was volatile, it was like Detroit. I carried a gun half the time I was in Detroit, until I got saved. I shot at people, I was one of them. I just wanted a change, I didn't want to go to Savannah and start fighting all over again."

So, he made another selection, and out of all the cities, he chose Albany, Georgia. As soon as he stepped off the plane his mind was made up. "When I came to Albany I had on a $10,000 coat, the day I left Detroit it was 10 degrees below zero, an ice storm. I left with my two sons, Tyrone and Buzzy. They had their coats on, and when we hit Tallahassee it was warm, and when we came to Albany it was hot, we were sold right there."

The acquisition of the Albany stores was completely uncomplicated. "We had a swap. Kentucky Fried Chicken and I just swapped like you trade cars without any money. They took the territory there which was a gold mine, and I took the territory here, which was a gold mine, and I moved to Albany, Georgia just on a swap." A sign that this was what he was supposed to do.

That acquisition was probably the only simple thing that has occurred to Brady since his arrival. Since settling in Albany he has faced conflict after conflict.

John Draper, Brady Keys, Jr., and Leonard Burnett made history by building the nations first and largest black owned Burger King chain starting in Detroit, MI.

114

Albany businessman Brady Keys, center, and his wife, Anna, left, receive the key to the city of Albany from Albany Mayor Tommy Coleman. The award recognizes Keys' 30 years of business in the city. He owns Kentucky Fried Chicken franchises and radio station WJIZ among others.

Brady in front of one of his blessings.

Keys speaks with actions but often is misunderstood

By JOHN RICHARDS
Herald Staff Writer

Albany businessman Brady Keys has an image problem.

Despite more than 25 years of helping other people while building his own multi-million dollar corporation from scratch, he says few people here understand him or his motivations.

"Being Brady Keys is very difficult in this town," he said in a recent interview. "There's always a story going around about me. I'm extremely misunderstood."

A former All-Pro defensive back for the Pittsburgh Steelers and one of the first blacks in the nation to become a major franchiser of fast-food restaurants, Keys said his success and visibility make him an enigma to both whites and blacks here.

"Who do you satisfy? How do you satisfy the people?" he asks.

Blacks often expect him to be their standard bearer — to use his wealth and prominence to lead the big causes they can follow along on, he said. "They want to claim victory with you."

Others in the black community assume, without getting to know him, that he has become too big and powerful "to relate to the little people," he said.

Keys said he's pretty much accepted by white society "because they think 'he's different, he's more like us,'" but that the acceptance is tenuous.

When he considered purchasing a home in Doublegate some years back, the story going around

See Keys, Page 11A

Chapter 26

A Rude Awakening

When I came down here I was already one of the top 100 Black Businesses, and here I came to this city that was racially polarized, and Blacks eat Blacks. The White man used Blacks as guard dogs. They sick Blacks on you, and they guard the wealth here by sicking Blacks on you, and they sat back and acted like they were not doing anything.

So, the guard dogs came after me here, they attacked me everywhere. I came here as a big business person, you could put all the Black businesses together here and they wouldn't have been half my size, and they still aren't. My thinking and my way of doing things was just unheard of in this area.

Brady's first conflict in Albany was with the owner of the daily paper, "The Albany Herald."

Mayor Gray controlled the town here, he owned everything, and he also owned "The Albany Herald." My first ad in the Albany Herald they didn't print. Their thinking was 'what the hell, who are you? We are just not going to print the ad', and I had paid for it.

So I called up and asked to speak to the owner. I didn't know it was Mayor Gray, I didn't really care. Everybody else tried to solve the problem, and I said I'm not going to talk to none of ya'll, you let me talk to whoever owns this damn place!

Finally I got to who owned it, and I jumped in his case. He laughed, and said "boy you are brave", and he said. "I'm going to fix the problem," and he did. I saw him out that night and everybody said that's Mayor Gray, and he's the most powerful man in town and he does this to people and he does that to people. So I went over and talked to him. I'm coming to a town where these people are afraid of this little man. I've spent time with the President of the United States, so how can I be afraid of this man?

I went up and told him about it, I said, "I'm sorry we had to have this fuss today, but you can't do that to me." He said "you're right, but I can't believe you are brave enough to come to me and say something about it."

I said, "Well I'm brave enough, and when I spend my money you've got to give me my ad, but I just wanted to come and apologize for being so nasty, but he couldn't stop laughing. I found out why he couldn't stop laughing because he couldn't believe I had the guts to do that."

Those guts have always brought Brady problems in Albany, and they are partially responsible for the reason he has never been completely accepted. However, he has not allowed the lack of acceptance hinder him from accomplishing the mission God has set forth for him in Albany, and his own personal objectives he set for himself.

"So when I came here I did what I said I was going to do, and I got involved with the Black college, Albany State University." Even though his intentions with the school was completely selfless, his reception from the college was no better than his initial reception from the Albany Herald.

"I got ready to give to the Black college and I said I'm going to give you money, but I need some conditions here. First of all, you don't have any White people here. I think you need White people on here for this team to get accepted. Second of all, I'm going to give to athletics, and you've got to get some White people. I'm going to give you scholarships for athletes because my theory is if you get a school that is doing great in athletics it attracts money from alumni, and others.

So I gave them $20,000 worth of scholarships. They were losing. They used that money to recruit and give scholarships to good players, including White people. But while I was up there giving them $20,000, they were giving me a ticket on my car downstairs trying to tow it away. I mentioned to the President, Billy Black, I said, "Look Billy you've got to take care of these tickets, I parked down here I had to park where I could," and he wouldn't do anything about it.

President Black never did, but Coach Hampton Smith was appalled by the incident and offered to pay for the ticket because Brady was adamant about not paying for it. Brady told them, "I'm not going to pay for the ticket, they can take my car if they want to, but I'm not going to pay for the ticket."

But that has been his relationship with Albany State, and with the city.

Brady and fellow KFC franchisee Milt Sanders visit with the Albany State Football players who each received one of the $20,000 in scholarships awarded by Brady Keys, Jr.

Chapter 27

KAB & WJIZ - Divine Intervention

Brady's entire life, since he was a young child who was constantly sick, has been filled with conflicts that have resulted in positive resolutions.

It seemed that the Steelers and or professional footballs' influence over Brady's life had ended. But it never really ends once you look at it. Once a professional football player, especially with a little flamboyance, you are always a professional football player. It seemed that Brady's relationship with the Steelers in general and Art Rooney Sr. in particular, continues to be a blessing.

Doron Levin, who at the time was a Bureau Chief for *Time Magazine*, saw Brady at an affair in Detroit. Doron came up to him and referred to Brady's good old days with the Steelers. One thing led to another but it was obvious that an everlasting friendship was established. Doron and Brady just got along and probably will always get along, so it would seem. Doron wanted Brady to meet one of his "special friends." He arranged a meeting with special friend Phil Handy. How could it be that Brady and Phil could possibly hit it off as good as Doron and Brady did. It is always a gamble when you introduce people, there is one thing that always lingers in the back of your mind, you always hope that the people being introduced would like to get along with one another. Well, Phil and Brady liked one another from the very start and they made a pledge to do business with one another.

Time passed... Phil and Brady barely stayed in touch but people who have met Brady and people who have had the opportunity to really get to know him rarely forget him and Phil had not forgotten Brady.

Soon after the sale of the Burger King restaurants Brady received another message from God saying "The Blessing Must Continue." Upon receiving this divine message, Brady got a call from Phil. There was a minority concession coming up in the Orlando International Airport in Orlando, Florida and Phil said "Brady, Orlando needs a businessman like you that happens to be Black. Come down to Orlando and let me introduce you to my friends and the people in the community." Phil also mentioned that he would put Brady in touch with the right people to talk too, as well as help him with the politics.

The business relationship brought to the forefront other blessings. Phil did not know he was God sent, no more than Art Rooney or any of the others involved with Brady's success. Larry Beiter, the first person who came to Brady in 1974 to suggest that he pursue an airport concession, which he and Brady established themselves as the first minority concession in America... Larry did not know he was "God sent" and a part of A.C. Franklin's prayer, neither did Detroit Metropolitan Airport Director, J. Norton know he was a part of the blessing when he gave Brady his "temporary" eight year verbal relationship to allow him to put his Polaroid Face Place machines in the Detroit Airport... and the list of blessings continue to flow on, even to Phil in Orlando... even to Irene Rios, "the hard to get" manager that Brady had to personally get to manage Keys News and Gift Shop.

"I knew we would win the concession at the Orlando Airport. However, I did not realize how political and how very difficult it is to win concessions at that airport. We had no experience at running a Gift Shop but business is business. When we missed a recent bid for a food concession after becoming the largest and highest volume minority News and Gift Shop in any airport in the nation... after that shocking loss, I realized I had to humble myself. Just being the best is not enough. Like Bill Jennings, Bill Miller, and Darryl Benton (officials at the airport) said to me after the ordeal "it takes four votes to get anything approved by the board at the airport." I realized then that just being the best is not good enough. God has to be in the plan."

His many life experiences have taught him to rely completely on God. As a result of those experiences, he has also learned to wait for God's instruction before he makes any major decisions, and he has learned to heed those messages, even if he doesn't agree with them or understand why they are to be. And that was certainly the case when he was approached about buying the urban radio station in Albany, WJIZ.

"I didn't want that station, I didn't want them to be in business at all. The city wanted me to have it. Rudy Goddard wanted me to have it because I was the only Black person who could get a loan large enough."

WJIZ was nothing but conflict for Brady, conflicts that began before he ever received official ownership. His problems with the station began with the process of financing the purchase.

"As soon as Security Bank decided to give me the loan they were getting pressure from other banks here. 'You don't want to give no nigger a $2 1/2 million dollar loan.'

That's a lot of money to people here, but $2 1/2 million dollars is nothing to me. I've gotten loans into the millions and millions and millions, but it was a lot of money for here. So, in the middle of the deal, Security Bank changed the terms on me, after I had gotten the station. I have forgiven them, but I have never forgotten it. The fact that they did that has been a major source of anger for me, but Security has done more for me than any bank ever."

With all the conflicts before the deal was finalized, Brady contemplated walking away from the deal several times, but a force greater than him prohibited him from doing that.

"The Lord spoke to me, in fact he spoke to my preachers. I was debating whether I should take it, and my preacher from Detroit, Pastor Andrew Merrit, called me, not even knowing what I was doing. And he said the Lord spoke to him, and told him that I should go forward with buying it, and he didn't even know anything about it. Then my pastor here at New Covenant, Larry Cornett, in the middle of church said, "Brady Keys I've got a message from the Lord for you. The Lord said for you to go forward and buy the station."

So, I got two preachers in different parts of the world, and here I am thinking about trying to get out of buying it. The Lord sends a message to them, and says you buy it, and one doesn't even know anything that is going on, and one had no knowledge of what I'm doing said the Lord spoke to me. So of course I proceeded to get it."

If that were not enough, the Lord sent him further confirmations that this is what he was suppose to do. "I spent a lot of money researching, but I told the Lord if you want me to have this you are going to have to just give it to me, because I don't want it, and that's exactly what he did."

Tommy Chatman and Larry Bays went and got Bobby Lee, the previous owner of Silver Star, who owned WJIZ, to sign a document. He was about bankrupt, but he still did not want to do it. They got him to sign it, they're the champions. Rudy Goddard convinced Security Bank to loan me the money, and they loaned me all the money. I didn't have to put up any money. The $2 million worth of debt that was on it, and the half a million dollars of working capital. Security Bank loaned me all that money, and even though they messed up by changing the deal, they still were champions along with Larry Bays and Tommy Chatman."

The conflict behind purchasing the station was just the beginning. Compared to the problems that awaited Brady once he assumed ownership of the station, that was just the tip of the Iceberg.

Besides the station itself having major financial problems, and being what he describes as an "immoral mess" with the stealing and nasty music, he was completely unprepared for the other troubles that awaited him.

"I had just sold my Burger Kings, and I had a tremendous amount of income coming in. I bought this house from this doctor, there were some really heavy negotiations, and I got the better of the deal. He went and told all the White people I stole it from him, which I did not. I just negotiated better.

Once I bought it, the White people would come through my yard, I had a big yard, and they would come through my yard sight seeing. There were 10-15 cars a day that would drive through there sight seeing, and that bothered me. One day, this tall, thin, heavily bearded, nasty White guy walked inside my house. I was sitting there looking at television, and there he was right behind me. He said, "Oh, this is how rich niggers live."

I said I have got to do something about this. I've got people coming all day, and this guy walked right in my house, people coming and wanting to borrow money, just all kinds of traffic to me once I got this house. God knew what I had to do, I built this fence around it, but it cost, it's extravagant.

I had a lot of money at the time, lots of money, and you've got a half a million dollar home, you don't want to build a 10 cent fence, especially Brady Keys the Black man moving into this high rich area. So I said, Brady you'd better not buy a cheap fence because they'll talk about you forever. So I decided to build an expensive fence and they talked about me forever.

He was on the front page of the Albany Journal three times, and the Albany Herald once for this extravagant, imported, $175,000 fence. He was also criticized for employing Black people to build it, but what they didn't know was that he had employed White people to put in the electrical systems. As a result, people would drive by and throw things at the Black employees who were building the fence. The papers reported that Brady Keys was fencing the White folks out.

That controversy sparked what was to become years of problems with the IRS.

"The IRS in Albany met with Larry Bays, and told him, we gonna get that nigger. We saw him when he bought WJIZ, and we didn't audit him. We really got upset when the radio station supported getting rid of the rebel flag, we still didn't audit him. And we didn't even audit him when he bought the big house and took it from the doctor. But when he built the fence and fenced the White folks out, it was time for him to be audited, and we're going to take him down. That's what they told Larry Bays. They said he's got $1.3 million in the bank, and we're going to take it all. We're going to audit until we get it all, and that's exactly what they did."

Although things were looking pretty bad for Brady, and he was saddled with a station that seemed to only cause him more problems, he would soon learn the purpose behind all of it.

"The Lord knew this was going to happen. I had a lot of income coming in, and I needed a way of sheltering it. He knew that they were going to audit me and take all my cash. A man with a lot of wealth, and is cash poor is the poorest man in the world because it takes more money to overcome your problems, and once you become cash poor, no banks will loan it to you."

With the IRS taking every cent of income he could acquire, the station became extremely valuable to Brady.

"I had all this cash coming in from Burger King, which I had to pay a lot of tax on. The audit by the IRS took more of my tax money. So theoretically I was broke, but I had WJIZ and WJYZ. I'm amortizing the purchase, and that amortization of the purchase freed up cash for me that the IRS couldn't touch. They tried to, but they couldn't touch it. So WJIZ was actually the thing that kept me alive during these terrible years with the IRS trying to take things from me.

To the day that the amortization ran out, to the year the amortization ran out, the Lord spoke to me, November 1996, he said Brady next year you sell the station, and I'll find you a buyer. And here comes the buyer, and I sold the station, but right at the end of this amortization that was protecting me, the amortization was all gone, and I sold the station ... more cash!"

When God was ready to reveal his purpose for the station, Brady realized the station was meant to be protection for him against all of his IRS problems, and he learned a very valuable lesson.

"That is why when bad things happen to me I don't despair, because out of conflicts come the answer to things, or come prosperity, but you've got to persevere and have faith."

Staff of Keys News and Gift Shop in Orlando International Airport.

Chapter 28

Acts of Faith

To many people unfamiliar with Brady's spirituality and tremendous faith, the events that have occurred in his life may seem surreal, but to Brady it is a lifestyle for which he has become accustomed.

He is very in tune with his spirituality, and he has allowed God to use him as a vessel to do his work. He has learned to let God direct his path, and since then, his life has become much simpler. Since he became saved, he has many examples of ways God has manifested in his life.

"In the last 15 years, God has given me so many insights I have actually started to write things down that he said were going to happen. The Burger King sell ... four months before it ever started I wrote Len, and I said Len we are going to sell the Burger Kings for a record number of dollars. He said "it will never happen, they're dead, we can't do it, we're in the inner city," this that and the other. I said, it's going to happen, but we have to tithe.

I started tithing. I tithed thousands of dollars a week. God said give the money to the church. I tithed so big from the company it was breaking us. But I remember this, the last time I tithed I gave $8,500 to the church. Len saw it, and he said "Brady you have tithed all of our money,' but we were in negotiations with Burger King. I said, Len something good is going to happen to us."

The next day, after I gave the $8,500, I gave it on a Sunday, and the next day, on Monday, the impossible happened. We got a call from Burger King, they had approved the deal, and closing was going to take place eminently. The odds of closing at all were 50 to 1 against us."

Brady has received several messages from God since he became saved. He has been described by those who are close to him as being gifted, in relation to being chosen to carry out

God's instructions. He has received many of his messages in different forms. Many have been in the form of dreams, and by way of messages through preachers, with the most blatant being from his two preachers who gave him the message to buy WJIZ.

As a result of his connection with God, Brady is adamant about not allowing anyone to interfere with his blessings.

"I tell people with me, if you just stick with me, and do what I ask you to do. You've got to get inside the blessing, and then ride the cloud. I've had to excommunicate people who were not inside the blessing. I'm very cold that way because if a person gets outside the blessing I must cut them away because they'll take me outside of it too. I know I'm protected as long as I do certain things. As long as I stay within the protectiveness of the spiritual realm of what I'm suppose to do. I cannot, and will not be stopped."

Brady congratulating Len Burnett on sticking with him for 30 years since their days as rookies with the Pittsburgh Steelers.

Chapter 29

Moving Forward

As soon as he received the word from God, Brady began to take the necessary steps to sell the station. Even though he always said he didn't want to be in the radio business, no one believed he would ever sell the station. After all, he'd turned the station into a gold mine. Under his reign the station went from being nearly bankrupt when he acquired it, to the #1 urban station in the country.

However, for Brady, life is a series of phases, and he says he is motivated by God. So, when God told him it was time to move on, that is exactly what he did. According to Brady, God told him to buy the station, and he also told him to sell it.

Before he could officially rid himself of WJIZ, he'd already begun to move forward to the next phase. On October 15, 1997 the selling of the radio station was official, and one month to the day, on November 15, 1997, Brady Keys, Jr., was in Atlanta, Georgia celebrating the pre-launch of his next business — Keys Group Marketing, Inc.

He has described this latest business venture as the most promising business venture he has ever embarked upon. "It has the greatest growth opportunity. It has unbelievable potential. It is frightening how big it can be," Brady said.

Brady Keys has been said to have the midas touch when it comes to running a business, but strangely enough with the exception of his chicken businesses, he has never entered a business with any special expertise in those fields. He knew nothing about burgers, radio, newspapers, or coal, and with his most recent company, he especially has absolutely no knowledge of computers. But he is the first person to tell you that there is one thing that he does know.

"All I know is how to run a business successfully." And according to Brady, that is all it boils down to, knowing how to run a business.

"The business of business is business. The principals of running a business are all the same: A+B=C. It doesn't change. You can put different numbers in there and different businesses in those categories, but the formula never changes."

After 30 years of successfully running numerous businesses, he certainly knows that of which he speaks. Brady has made fortune after fortune in his lifetime, and he prides himself on the ability to have done so without the benefit of a fancy education, and that he has done so by applying the same formula time after time after time.

Keys Group Marketing is a multi-level marketing company. Although Brady is not certain of the purpose for his new company, he is certain that it is the right thing to do.

"I don't know where it fits, but I know there is something that God wants me to do here. I believe it is one of these divine things, although I never received any word that it was, but I can see how it's developing like all these other things."

Brady especially feels he has a divine purpose because this particular field, the high-tech business and computer technology, is of no interest to him at all. "I hate computers because I believe they are the instrument of the destruction of the world. I believe they are the catalyst for the control of people, the 666, everything."

In addition to his theory, he has no skills of knowledge of computers, which he attributes to his mother. "My mother told me very early, and it kind of ruined me, not to do anything with my hands. Always use my brains, then I can make enough money and find somebody that can do it with their hands. She told me she said, you think hard, and you out think everybody, and out think your problems. As a result, I never learned a computer, I never learned typing, I never

131

learned anything. I don't change tires, I don't do anything with my hands, but I do know how to think really well."

He has no knowledge of computers, but he knows it is imperative to change with the times. So, when the opportunity presented itself he jumped on the bandwagon. The way in which he became involved in this new venture was partly by chance and by being in the right place at the right time.

"Jerome Hughes got in touch with Adrienne Archie trying to talk to me. I don't let people come directly to me, I make them talk to some of my people. So Adrienne came to me and she said here's a machine that will get you on the internet. She came with this machine that had a keyboard, I didn't touch it. So then she came back to me, she said they have video conferencing. I said oh, I can hook all my restaurants together, and then I can save money, I'm interested."

Once he was interested. Jerome Hughes and Katrina Greenhill came to Albany to meet him, and to make their presentation to him. He was sold, he got involved, and made a lot of money, so the next step was to take Jerome and Katrina to Orlando to make a presentation to Brady's business partner, Len Burnett, and that is when things began to change.

"After the presentation, which was successful, we all went to my condo. We were sitting around the table eating, and the conversation came up about the internet. As I listened to them talk about the internet, and as I listened to Jerome talk about the multi-level marketing system, I said to them, I see something. I'm always looking for the impossible, and something that has never been done. I said, we need to be able to make websites that everybody is talking about like a McDonald's makes hamburgers, or Burger King. Burger King not necessarily because they have it your way. McDonald's don't let you have it your way, they take it and make it cheaper, but they make it one way. They make it fast, and they sell a lot of them.

I said, we need to do something that has never been done. We need to make websites for under $200 that ordinarily cost between $2000-4,000. I said 'Wynn can you do it.' He said "I think I can."

"I got involved with this company because I was sitting one evening with Mr. Keys, and I had just finished designing a website for him. I told him that we could take this website, and sell it to thousands and thousands of people in different multi-level marketing companies. That gave him an idea, and he wanted to know how I could do that for such a reasonable price. I told him because it's a template, and all the works done. Now just change the name, their address, their e-mail account, their I.D. number, and that takes very little time, and you can sell them a $2,000 and $3,000 website for a couple of hundred dollars," Wynn recalled.

Brady continued, I then said, Jerome if we can make those websites for under $200, can your multi-level marketing people see them, and he said Absolutely!"

Jerome explained his motivation for getting involved with this new venture.

"I left my previous business to start this venture, and the purpose for that is because I see a much bigger picture here with Mr. Keys versus what I was doing. I was very successful with what I was doing, but long term I think this will be much more rewarding, not only for me, but for people that get involved."

After everyone stated their interest in embarking on this new business, they then began to put their plans into action to formulate the company, and that was the birth of Keys Group Marketing.

They didn't know very much at that time, all they had was a good idea, but Brady knew they had to establish two important things. The first thing being that he would have controlling interest, and secondly, "We are going to base this on Christian principle."

When they began to question where they would get the people to do the things they had proposed, Brady had no concerns about where the people would come from. In all his business dealings, and his most successful ventures, the people have always been directed to him by a power much greater than he.

"I have never gone after anything, or anybody. They are all sent to me. They all come, everybody, everything comes. I keep telling them, if you don't know why you are here, if you pray you'll understand why you are here. You are sent to me for me to accomplish what God wants me to accomplish."

And since the development of Keys Group Marketing that is exactly what has happened. Every product they have needed has been acquired, and all done by people who came to them, people they did not go out to get.

"Wynn said he could do it, but he had no software to do it with because you can't do it on any of the software that is available today, at least that we knew about. Guess what happened? Here comes a company called "Inca" out of the clear blue."

Inca had the software that Keys Group Marketing needed to develop their websites. Inca was making templates for hospitals, and they were able to store them in the software.

And according to Brady, "Then you can reach and pull them out and get colors, music, and all kinds of things. That gave us the ability to make web pages in minutes."

That is a prime example of how life is for Brady, but that was only the beginning. Since then they have been presented with similar opportunities, which have allowed the company to become high-tech. Dr. Francis Palmera, a computer genius, was also brought into the company without knowledge of why he was even there.

"He just came to us, and now he is helping us put this whole thing together. He has invented the software for the internet telephone, and he has made it available to us. The internet telephone is a brand new invention, and he cut the software ... all of a sudden, we are high-tech that quick. With one product we changed from a regular multi-level

134

company to a high tech company," Brady explained.

"Our technology is based on the idea that dreams do come true, and to help people to succeed is pretty much our business. I believe we are on a mission of God," Palmera explained.

The events that have transpired thus far may be questioned by some, and seem to be almost miraculously but not to Brady. "I expect God to bring things to me. If I start to question it as too good to be true. I'm not in line, or in the stream for a blessing. When you're not in the spiritual realm, you look at things as too good to be true. If you are in a spiritual realm you expect things to happen. I expect more things to happen."

Chapter 30

Remembering Brady

Maxine Willis
Detroit, Michigan

Mr. Keys is a phenomenal man. I have watched him deal with the bum on the street, and I have watched him deal with the highest level in Washington, D.C. He is a person who exemplifies what he says. You hear people say he walks the walk, and he talks the talk, and that's why I will stand behind him until the end, because he truly believes in his message. The exciting thing about what is happening now is that dream is going to be disseminated throughout the country, more people exposed to him. He is the kind of person that is willing to share his knowledge, his resources, and will prepare you. I feel like I have gone through a Ph.D in business administration from Mr. Keys. But the greatest thing I'd like to say about him is we certainly want to keep the tradition, the history of Keys Group philosophy alive, and I think it is certainly going to have an impact on children of the future.

R.J. Watkins
Owner TV studio (TNVC)
Detroit, Michigan

He's the reason I'm doing what I'm doing now. Mr. Keys invested $250,000 in me about 5 years ago, and it was a free high deal. Basically, we had a Christmas party one day, and he asked me what I wanted for Christmas. I told him I don't know. He said, "I know what I'm going to buy you for Christmas." I said, what's that Mr. Keys. He said, "I'm going to get you that TV studio you always wanted. My mouth fell open, he said come talk with me after the holidays, and get with Burnett, and get your staff list, and I'm going to get the studio for you. And true enough, by my birthday, which was June 22 of that year, June 23 we closed the deal. Mr. Keys has been very good to me.

Robert Sims
Medical Doctor
Detroit, Michigan

I've known Brady for about 20 years, we met at a basketball game. He's an astute businessman, and an untiring, successful person. There's nothing plastic about Brady Keys, and what you see is what you get.

Dan Rooney
President of Pittsburgh Steelers

It is with pleasure to say nice things about Brady Keys. He was a fine football player for the Steelers, and always carried himself with character, dignity, and with good humor.

Brady was always a person that looked at the whole picture while playing. He also considered his life after football, and examined various business opportunities, and worked to that end. He did become a successful business person.

My father, Arthur J. Rooney, was very fond of Brady, and they would talk about business, and other things including Brady's family. Brady Keys raised his family, and they are all a credit to him and society.

Mary Wiley
Former Employee of WJIZ
Albany, Georgia

God has always shown me to look at him as a "King". I mean in the sense of going back to the Old Testament. He's full of wisdom. I really truly believe God has anointed him with the gift to prosper.

Since I have left him I can see that working directly with the owner was such a blessing, and now I see the value of working with him. Working with Mr. Keys you can go directly to him, there is no middle man to go between.

When God touches our lives it doesn't matter what kind of person you are. No matter what kind of things he does outside of what he was called to do, he still has that gift to prosper. For some people who know Mr. Keys, all they can see is the man, but I was able to get to know "the man of God."

Toby Bryant
Early Childhood Friend

I knew Brady Keys when he was going to Polytechnic High School and I was going to Emmanuel Hearts we became very good friends there. During high school for about three years he was an excellent football player and from there he escalated his skills after he left high school. I went into the service and when I came back I got into the real estate business. I recall him retiring from football then he went full time into the chicken business and there his success was very inspiring. He has escalated to Radio Stations. I went to Albany, Georgia with him and I was down there for a few months. The chicken business was great and his radio station turned out real good. He's been very successful. Brady is a fantastic businessman.

Marvin Wilford
Childhood Friend
Austin, Texas

Brady and I started off in the first grade together at LL Campbell School. Brady didn't have any brothers and sisters and I didn't either, so we were always real close. We went through football together from junior high to high school. Brady was always a person that had the will to go a head and do what he needed to do. He would do anything in the world that he could for you. The first year of high school we played one year of football together and then the doctor told him that he couldn't play football because he had a bad heart. Brady had a determination to go on and do it. He left with his Mother and went to California and he did real well out there. Lawrence Brown keeps me up to date on Brady. When Brady made the Hall of Fame

Lawrence sent me some pictures and wrote me a letter. Brady is a swell guy and I'll always love him. He will always be in my heart. Lawrence wrote me a letter and said that we were crazy for hitting those guys in school because we were so little and the other guys were so big, but we did it.

Diane Gillette-Clark
Former Employee of WJIZ
Albany, Georgia

In the six years that I had the opportunity to work, and get to know Brady Keys, Jr., I have learned a lot about business. I have to say he is a visionary that can take something, and study and develop business opportunities to their full potential. Mr. Keys gathers knowledge and puts together a business plan that makes sense. Once the plan is developed he looks for the best people to carry out the business plan. He relies a lot on this wonderful, God given instinct. When an opportunity presents itself, he will pray about it, and ask for the Lord's direction to ensure that the endeavor is pleasing to the Lord.

One of the other wonderful things about Mr. Keys is his genuine interest about his employees. He will work closely to teach, train, and develop his people. You always know when you're doing a good job ... or when you messed up ... because he'll tell you straight up!!! He believes in his people and studies their capabilities to develop their potential. He's tough, he expects a lot, but he rewards accordingly. No, let me correct that ... VERY generously.

Mr. Keys is about PRINCIPLES, no not the school kind ... PRINCIPLES. Probably the highest stand that sticks out with me is how he feels about youth, and what we do that can effect them. At Keys Airport Business prior to the store opening, he told a magazine representative that he wasn't interested in selling the magazines that needed a brown wrapper to hide the cover. The rep couldn't believe he would turn down the dollars the magazine would generate. But Mr. Keys was concerned they might fall into some small hands, or the wrappers wouldn't cover. He just didn't want the sales from the "adult magazines." At Keys Communication, WJIZ he refused to accept parental advised lyrics, and sent the music back to the record companies. He coordinated gun buy backs to get the illegal weapons off the streets twice in Albany, Georgia, and once in Orlando, Florida.

I'm just happy that the Lord put me in the right place at the right time, and I had the wonderful Keys experience!!! It has truly been a blessing!!!

Don Harty
Charisma Group Burger King stores
Harlem, New York

I was 20 years old in the fall of 1977 when I first met Brady. I would not be where I am today if it were not for Brady. He gave me my first big break into franchising when no one else would! He sold me my first store at a fraction of the blue book cost because the store was closed, and he wanted to get it off his hands. I couldn't believe it, so I bought it!

I remember I owed Brady a substantial amount of money, but I just couldn't find the funds to pay him. I was flat busted! Well, some of his people were acting like prudent business people ... they wanted to sue me!! Brady said, "No! We can work something out ... and we did. Brady backed me up all the way ... 100%! What can you say about a person like that? He taught me how to give something back to the community.

Tom Reich
Former Partner - All-Pro-Chicken

One of the key reasons for our success was Brady. He had a tremendous amount of energy and burr. He could charm the pants off a man or woman, and the fact that he was a celebrity professional football player helped too.

We both possessed special skills. I was trained in finance, legal, and well versed in business in general. We most definitely complemented each other. The world knew that we were a winning combination, which enabled All-Pro to attract some pretty big fish who admired our zeal, savvy, and nobility. They knew our climb would be a rough uphill struggle to the top of the crest. Moreover, the million dollar question was ... was the world ready for Brady Keys, Jr? The times were hateful! It was an era of change. Whether the world was ready for Brady or not, it didn't make a difference because Brady Keys, Jr., was ready for the world.

Walter Thomas
Former Board member of All-Pro Fried Chicken
The good reputation that I have earned today is a direct consequence of my relationship with Brady. People still come to me because they know that it was guys like me and Brady who were out front.

Joseph R. Wilson
Networker, Keys Group Marketing
After meeting Mr. Brady Keys it was his genuineness, his very sincereness, what he felt for the African American community, and how he wanted to share his success with that community. I have not ever met anybody of his stature that was so personable and sincere.

I think he's a great guy, I think he's fabulous, he's a tremendous individual. With his business acumen, you can see his success. You know that success would easily follow with just his personality, and sincereness. I know a lot of people with money, but Mr. Keys is exceptional.

Wynn E. Miller
Co-Founder Keys Group Marketing
Orlando, Florida
I've known Mr. Keys since 1991. I've been making puppets for over 25 years, and he has been buying them from me since 1991. My impression of Mr. Keys is he's the most honest businessman I have ever run into. In fact, I use to always talk about other people I do business with, or associate with, saying that I have a company called Keys Group at the Orlando Airport that I've never had a

141

problem collecting money from for my merchandise. In fact, sometimes they have even given me the money before the merchandise, and asked me to store merchandise for them if I needed the money. So, I found they were one of the best people I've worked with.

Stephanie Hawke
Sales Representative for TCI Cable (8 year client)
Albany, Georgia

My first impression of Mr. Keys was, I was impressed that someone that famous, and powerful lived here in southwest Georgia. I'd heard about him, that he owned KFC stores, and he was a former Pittsburgh Steeler, and I wanted to set up an appointment with him. I'd heard that he spends time in the restaurants, so I went to the restaurant. He was having lunch, and I went over and sat down with him, he bought me soup.

What has always impressed me about Brady is his ability to be talking to New York on the phone, sitting there looking at a picture of Bill Cosby on his desk, his wife on the other phone, and doing business with me at the same time. He never gets rattled, he is very multi-tasked. He can do several things at one time. He can get people to do things they don't even know they're doing, and make them want to do it.

If you don't know him you'd think he was this tough, big businessman, but he is just a teddy bear on the inside. A lot of people that don't know him would think, oh Brady Keys is this big community leader, tough business executive. He's just a puppy dog ... a very smart, successful, puppy dog!!

Chapter 31

Born Again

I was baptized in Austin, Texas at Ebenezer Baptist Church. I will never forget my baptism, because it was the wrong time. As a child, my mother would say, "Boy, when you turn thirteen, unless you're baptized, your soul will go straight to the devil!"

I would be out late riding my bicycle all over the place. I was never concerned about my soul because I wasn't thirteen yet, and I knew if something happened to me my soul would go straight to heaven. When I became thirteen, I started to worry about my soul. Then the day finally came for me to go to church and get baptized. What a chore. I had to sit up front on the mourners bench. The baptists made a big spectacle of it. The fact that my soul was going to go to hell made me go through with the arduous task of joining the church!

I remember riding on the bus with a white sheet on, on my way to the river. All the little old ladies were mourning, crying, and praying for us, flapping their heavy arms in the air, joyful that we finally decided to return our souls to the LORD. Hah! While me and another young boy were just cracking up!

It was such a BIG joke to us to see them rocking back and forth, shouting, "JESUS! YES LORD!!" We laughed to ourselves all the way to the river. The preacher was a burly, Black man with a thunderous voice that seemed to go right through you.

I remember being just a little bit frightened when he placed his wide hand on my head. Everybody was singing those old time southern spirituals, they began to jump up and down, filled with the holy ghost, shouting! Then, before I knew it, I was under water. It was just like when Jesus was baptized by John the Baptist! And when it was over, we went and played in the sandbox. So now I was baptized, from that point on I knew I had done the right thing. My soul was saved, Jesus would surely get it.

As I grew older my spiritual needs changed. I wasn't satisfied with Ebenezer Baptist Church any longer, so I moved on from church to church to church. Never really finding a good church that I could call my own, that I could call home! Before I knew it, thirty years had passed. I was busy living my life, but I still hadn't found a church that gave me gratification.

Anna, myself, and my kids then moved to Georgia. Then my mother also moved to Georgia. I had a nephew named Mark Shaw. He was a very, very, bad boy, until he had a spiritual awakening, and began to speak in tongues. When my mother told me of this, I thought it was funny because I had never heard of this. Speaking in tongues? What's that?

I didn't pay much attention to it, but when I saw how Mark had went through this metamorphosis I was positively amazed! He went from a reckless, troubled youth, to a religious, humble, peaceful, young man that had found his place in life through Christ. I didn't laugh so much anymore. I talked to Mark many times thereafter about the Holy Spirit that he so eagerly received. As far as God, and our family was concerned, Mark was a blessed person.

It didn't take long for my mother to start talking to me about finding a good church home that satisfied all my spiritual needs. I began to pray, I mean really talk with my LORD, and ask him to direct me to a church home.

In the meantime, I continued to attend different churches. Then one night I had a visit from what I positively believed was a divine spirit. It was just a peaceable experience. I felt good, real good afterwards.

It came into my room one night and spoke to me just as clear. It said my daughter, Yvette, would come to Georgia and live. I didn't understand this because I knew how my daughter felt about coming to Georgia ... she loathed the idea!

Two days later, my son-in-law called and said that he wanted to come to Georgia to live. I told him that I wasn't surprised. I then told him of the visit that I had from the spirit. My daughter,

Yvette, called me later and told me that she would have to pray about the decision, and she would call me back.

About a week later, she called me back, and said the Lord confirmed that she must go and live in Georgia. The Lord does indeed work in mysterious ways. When Yvette and her family came to Georgia one of the first things that she did was to search for a good Christian church home.

It didn't take long for her to find a church called: New Covenant Church. Yvette, staunch in religious faith, she would come over to the house and lay her hands upon me, and pray over me. I didn't understand what she was doing.

I went to visit the church several times, I enjoyed the services so much that I became a member. New Covenant was then, and still is today, a good church. I learned so much about the Lord, and how he wanted us to live on earth, and in his Kingdom. But again, I still wasn't totally spiritually fed, and I wasn't really involved with the church. I wanted to share with the church my gifts and my abilities. I wanted a relationship with the church, and New Covenant did not fill that need.

A few years later, in Detroit, I was sitting in my office when the phone rang. Keep in mind, it is very difficult to get directly to me, you must first go through my private secretary. Anyway, I picked up the phone, it was this preacher named Rev. Andrew Merritt from Straight Gate Church.

I had never heard of this man, or his church. I said, what can I do for you? He told me with great authority that the Lord told him to call me! I said, Brady if the Lord told somebody to call you, then you better listen! So I asked him, "well if the Lord told you to call ME, what did the Lord tell you to say?"

Rev. Merritt said that he had a package, and a church that he wanted to buy. He said, the Lord told him to buy it. But when it didn't look like it was going to happen, he started praying. He said that as he was driving his car, the Lord revealed to him MY name … Brady Keys, Jr., and that I would be the one to finance his church.

I said, "wait a minute! I DON'T finance no churches, I don't know anything about it. I tell you what, send me the package."

He personally hand carried the package to the office, and tried to see me, but I was busy so I didn't see him. He left his package with my secretary. I didn't even read the package. I sent it, along with a letter to my banker, Mr. Ed LeFevre, President of National Bank of Royal Oak, and a dear friend.

Ed LeFevre called on a business matter, he was helping me finance a Burger King. He made mention of the letter, and package. Ed wanted to know what exactly did I want him to do with the package ... look at it or what? He asked if I was endorsing the package. I told him to look at the package, and see what he could do with it. He told me that they didn't finance churches, and was I going to sign for this guy? I told him, "No! I don't even know the guy."

He said, "look Brady, you sent me the package, are you recommending him or what?" I didn't want to kill the deal for the church, so I just let things stand. So you see, I can't say that I really did anything to help the church get financed.

I received another call from Ed LeFevre, and to my surprise, I learned that Rev. Merritt had in fact called and told Ed the same story he told me. Needless to say, my banker and I were equally shocked. Rev. Merritt was a man of great tenacity. To make a long story short, the bank sent a team down to inspect the church that Rev. Merritt wanted to purchase, although they didn't finance churches, they looked at it, and you know what? They financed the church!

Well, everything went great, Rev Merritt got his church. I didn't know if he had got the financing or not, until I started getting these phone calls from this preacher again.

This time I didn't accept the calls. However, he kept on calling me, and my secretary, Charliene Snay, "Charlie" was getting downright tired of taking his calls. She then informed me that the church wanted to present me with an award. I didn't want any award, but Charlie was on my back, so I just told her to make a date ... any date. She made the date about six weeks in advance, on a Sunday, of course I had no intention of accepting that award.

I didn't give that engagement a second thought, until Charlie reminded me of the event that Friday. I still wasn't going!

The following Saturday night, I had been out all night checking on my Burger King stores. Man, I was dog-tired. All I wanted to do was sleep. Sunday morning stared me right in the face ... I just couldn't sleep! Something kept nagging at me. Every time I tried to dose off, I would just wake up. I said, "Lord! What's wrong with me? Why can't I get to sleep? Something keeps waking me up!"

Discombobulated, I then decided to call the church and let them know that I would be there to accept the award. The church answered the phone. I didn't find anything unusual about that, not until I found out what had transpired. The congregation was engrossed in prayer. They were immersed in prayer because the Lord had spoken to Rev. Merritt, and told him that I was thinking about not attending service. So they concentrated all their thoughts on me, asking the Lord to have me call. They turned the answering machine off, because they knew that I was going to call ... and I did!

I informed Rev. Merritt that I would be there at 11:00, but he advised me to come about 11:45. They wanted service to be further along, and everyone seated when I walked in the sanctuary.

I was prompt, the church was beautiful. I would learn later that the building was worth over $4 million, and it was sold for a mere fraction of the cost. It was hard to believe, Straight Gate Church was only four years old, from humble beginnings a few years ago as a meager storefront church. They had moved four times, in four years, and now they would never have to move again ... so I thought.

I was rather taken to see that the preacher was so young. It looked like the place was ran by children, I thought. I took my seat in the second row. When that man started to preach, all my doubts were put to rest. From that moment on, the Lord commenced to work with me. My prayers were delivered to me ... right in front of my eyes, my prayers were answered. I prayed for a church that I could be involved in, one that I could help personally ... Straight Gate was it! I prayed for a preacher that I could really relate to ... Straight Gate had one!

147

My mother often warned me to beware of preachers that strayed from the scripture, that made up things! This young man read straight from the text. He could teach, and preach ... he could preach and teach. It became crystal clear to me, he made my soul swell! I became so full of the spoken word. I wanted to burst with joy!

Before the end of the service, I had made up my mind ... this was the church for me, and I was going to become a member. When he asked if there were any people that wanted to join the church, that was my cue to stand. I tried to move my feet, and it seemed like the carpet was ten feet high, and I couldn't step over it. The Lord had other plans for me. I tried with all my strength to move ... and I couldn't. Finally, I just surrendered myself to Jesus, and let me tell you ... he took total control over my mind, and body.

I heard the minister say that regular service had concluded, but to wait. He wanted to introduce the church to Brady Keys, Jr., the man responsible for getting the church financed. He called me up to the pulpit, the spell was broken ... I could finally move my feet again, but I had no control over what came out of my mouth. I walked up to him, and he embraced me. The first thing that I heard come out of my mouth was ... "THE LORD HAS GOT A MESSAGE FOR YOU TODAY."

I couldn't believe what I was saying! It just came out! You are talking about a man that is always in control. I held the mike, and said, "You must wait on the Lord. What you pray for you must have faith to wait on. I stand here today before you as living proof of that prayer. The Lord surely will deliver."

I told the church how for years, I've prayed for a worthy church home. I then made a special request. I asked the church if I could have their permission to join Straight Gate Church. The response was incredible! The church went crazy. The minister at this point intervened, "Brady Keys, you wish to become a member of this church?" I said, "yes sir."

"Have you ever been baptized?" he asked. I said, "yes sir, as a child, but it wasn't the real thing."

"Have you ever spoken in tongues?"

I said, "no." In a soft, but firm voice he spoke these words that I will never forget as long as I live. "I am going to pray for you. All the members of the church will pray, and point their fingers at you, and when I tell you to speak, you WILL speak in tongues."

I said, "ok". Suddenly, I felt myself growing small, like I was fading away. I kept repeating over and over again to myself, "Brady, don't fall! Don't fall Brady! Don't fall!"

The church continued to pray with their arms outstretched. I could feel the power of their prayers. I then felt the awesome power of the Holy Ghost as it descended upon me. I then heard the minister say, "SPEAK! In the name of Jesus!" he bellowed.

I commenced to speak in tongues. I didn't realize that there was a man standing behind me, ready to catch me if I were to fall. The church had videotaped the blessed event. When I saw the tape, I could clearly see myself under the influence of the Holy Ghost!

It was incredible! I NEVER thought in a thousand years this would happen to a man like me! On that day, I was actually born again ... witnessed by all of Straight Gate, I was delivered unto a benevolent revelation, that fortified my faith that God almighty, all powerful creator of things both great and small is alive in the world, and in me. And when my body is laid to rest, I pray that the Lord shall prepare a place for me in his Kingdom!

Brady Bits
by Brady Keys Jr.

For Your Business & For Your Life

Recorded by Adrienne V. Archie

1. "The Greatest Thing God Ever Blessed Me With Was Nothing"
2. "You Have To Be Prepared To Lose A Deal To Make A Deal"
3. "The Business of Business is Business, It's Never Personal"
4. "If You Let The People Lead You, They Will Follow You Anywhere You Want Them To Go"
5. "Never Bank With A Bank, Always Bank With A Banker"
6. "Never Worry About Things That Are Out Of Your Control"
7. "Figure A Way To Figure It Out, It's The Difference Between Success And Failure"
8. "Actions Are First Thoughts, Be Careful What You Think About, The Less They Turn Out To Be Actions"
9. "Do Not Allow Your Mind To convince You To Settle For The C Zone (Comfort Zone, Excuses or Reasons) Focus on Success"
10. "If You Have Failed At Your Job, You Have To Develop A System"
11. "You Don't Manage People, You Manage Systems, So When Something Goes Wrong, You Correct The System, Not The People"
12. "The Older We Get, The Smarter Our Parents Become"
13. "Always Base Your Decisions On The Facts, Not Assumptions"
14. "Deliver On All Promises And Be Known For It By Your Clients"
15. "Anticipate And Eliminate Problems Before They Develop"

16. "Listen 90% Of Every Conversations With A Client; Ask Question 5%; Ask For The Order 5%"
17. "Excuses And Reasons Are Signs Of Nonperformance"
18. "The Name Of The Game Is, Get It Done"
19. "You Must Learn To Out Think Your Problems"
20. "Always Plan Your Week And Work Your Plan"
21. "If You Surround Yourself With Good People, You will Be A Great Leader"
22. "Your Greatest Asset Is Also Your Greatest Liability"
23. "Don't Be Satisfied With Coming Close, Be Satisfied With Coming In First"
24. "Do Not Take Rejection Personally, The Word No Can Mean Many Different Things"
25. "Selling Is Easy, You Don't Sell The Product, You Sell Yourself"
26. "When You Look The Part And Act The Part, You Are Looking And Acting The Part Of Success"
27. "Time Is Of The Essence And The Essence Of Time Is To Act Now"
28. "Live Up To The Principle Of Return On Investment Of Your Time By Not Wasting It"
29. It Takes Just As Much Time And Effort To Make $1,000,000.00 As It Does To Make $100.00"
30. "Pray Each And Everyday Before You Start Your Day And Ask God To Grant You Favors With Man … In His Son, Jesus, Name. Then Have Faith And Expect Favor.
31. "Never Ask For Things, Always Ask For Forgiveness … In Business.
32. "You don't have to be the greatest but you have to be the greatest at **TRYING** to be the greatest."
33. "You don't have to believe in **GOD** … but if you don't is the alternative really worth it?"
30. "Love is like a butterfly. You catch a butterfly real carefully so you will not crush it. Once you yield to temptation to look as it is flies away. *You grab love and once you open your heart it* (your love) *flies away.*

Epilogue

by Brady Keys, Jr.

All good things must come to an end, and so we come too hastily to a close. As I reflect back on my life, it is amazing to see the history that has been made through the Keys Group Company.

I started out poor, in regards to money, but I was always rich in the love that I had from my family, especially my mother. I can't tell the world enough how much I love that dear lady. Hungry, in terms of food for the spirit. What my very soul yearned for was a way out of poverty. When I was a mere child, I mean at eight, I knew what I wanted to be!

Those old days were the very, very, best days of my life. We never went hungry. We ate syrup and bread, sweet water, and red beans and rice. I loved it! I thank God for making me strong, both mentally and physically. I thank God for allowing me one pair of shoes because it has taught me to admire what I have. I thank him for not having any toys to play with as a child, because creating, making up my own games sharpened my mind into who I am today.

I didn't receive my first pair of "dress pants" until I graduated from junior high school. I was the only kid on the block to have black dress pants, and the one person who everybody thought wouldn't have on dress pants. My mother provided for me, and I was the only one that wore black dress pants in the whole neighborhood to the graduation.

So many times, doctors told me I wouldn't be able to play football because I had a bad heart. I just refused to believe that there was anything wrong with my heart. I just put it in the Lord's trusting hands, and he took care of it. He led me through twenty five years of athletic stardom, in not just football, but baseball and track. All praises go to God almighty!

I was not a very good student in my school days. It was really difficult adjusting from high school to college. I failed, and was lifted up again, given another chance, but I stumbled again. I never received a formal college degree. I have earned a degree from the college of the world, provided from the dean of all deans ... my LORD. I can certainly teach the teachers about the subject of business, and motivating people.

I remembered I injured my eye and skull in an exhibition game in my rookie year in professional football with the Pittsburgh Steelers. Again, I was told my career was over ... absolutely finished. They didn't know that God had a mission for me, a plan, and he saved my sight, my career, EVERYTHING, and he is still saving me today! Thank you sweet Jesus!

I can still vividly remember this miracle that only God could have performed. We were flat busted, out of money, nobody to turn to, up against a cold brick wall. I didn't worry then, and I'll not ever worry about my business because I know the Lord will provide. God had told me through the signs that my company was his, so I had nothing to fear. We didn't have the money to make payroll. Everybody was walking around in circles, but when Friday came, we had hard cash to pay all our debts.

The Lord knows the single biggest fear that I have is that my sons will fall out of the grace of God, and he will remove the veil of protection which has protected my dream from certain death.

I have allowed this book to be written to show the world that if you first put God in front of you, trusting him, and only him, by faith you will conquer all. I give God all credits because all credits are due unto him, for it was the wisdom that God bestowed upon me to record my works so that others may be inspired to work hard on their dreams.

I don't want to leave you bored with faceless statistics, or with cold empty words that have no real value or meaning. I most certainly would like to conclude this book on a high, positive note. Filling you up with pleasant, warm thoughts. Leaving you teeming, washed in the spirit. I have allowed this book to be written as a testimonial, a tribute to change. For there is nothing constant in the universe except change. You have seen the facets of my life. The baby, the boy, the MAN. I have done many things, some good, some bad. I have crossed many roads, some smooth, others thorny. A sundry of parts have I played. The many, many people I have come to know along the way, without ever truly knowing who Brady Keys, Jr., was, or what my life really stood for.

I have found myself at long last through him, Jesus Christ! Jesus has lifted me, elevated me to a higher ground, and yet I still struggle to prove to the Lord my love for him. I feel his love within, for that is the evidence that I did continue to achieve, which to this very day is a miracle.

Things that really made me seethe don't bother me anymore. When folks steal from me, I mean BLOOD! When they steal from the till I don't panic or go into a frenzy. I just go and open that till up a little wider, you see I give on my own free will, but by my terms, my conditions. When so-called good friends talk me down, I pray for them. So they might get busy with their time, using it in a positive way.

I've been in business for 31 years. I've seen businesses come and go. It seems rather strange, in my struggles to build the Keys Group empire, I've often had bitter conflict with those on the darker side of friendship. They somewhere along the road sought to do me dirt. I mean to sling it right in my eyes! Aha, how time has a way of telling on you. One, by one, those that sought malice against me are either out of business, or currently going out of business, defeated by God through me. I don't wish misfortune on anybody! It's a fact, when I find out there's trouble on the blocks hotline, I get right on it. If you could just see the shock, the dismay on their faces when they see that it is Brady Keys that comes to their rescue! Why? Because I'm a BIGGER man, in the spiritual sense! I don't hold a grudge, instead, I plant seeds of goodwill.

It is understood from the heart at Keys Group that we give genuinely, with a free hand. It is such a great feeling to share and be kind to folk. If you just get in the habit of doing good, goodness will follow you around like a bright shiny penny. Yes, you have to beware of the "takers" and "beggars". That is why we give to those who do not ask, we decide who is in need. At Keys Group Company, we give a hand! not a hand out.

You might say, that's nothing new, people have been killing each other from the very beginning. The first recorded murder, when Cain slew his brother Abel. That's nothing new! What is new is ... US! We weren't around in the beginning, but we are here now. Time is at hand. Seek the Lord while he may be found, call upon him while he is near. (Isaiah 55:6)

Heed his call, seek sanctuary in the Lord Jesus, while he is near. We are living in some crazy times. No longer is there right or wrong. Too many who choose to live only by the sword of lawlessness.

What will this world be like in the next 20 years for our children? Those precious little babies that you mother's cuddle and kiss. How many of them will die needlessly from the dope man's dirty needle? Or by the hands of another youth with flashy dreams living in a quick, instantaneous, polarized world, where the only thing that is certain is DEATH.

Mothers, fathers, if you really love your children like you think, GET UP! We've got to lick this thing together. When the life expectancy of the average Black male is seventeen years old, we've got to get moving and change things.

If we don't start right now to change things for our children, I mean make a concentrated effort, exhausting all our human resources to reroute the destructive path of our youth, then we have failed shamefully in the sight of God. We have not done our duty as true loving Christians. Children, especially my own, "Do as I say, and not as I do." The devil is in his final days, so he is very busy turning as many souls against God as he can. Do good in the site of God, and surely he shall have mercy on you.

When my fleshly body is laid to rest, I would hope to be remembered like the weeping willow. The weeping willow tree has a strong, yet graceful elegant beauty. It emanates a distinct flavor of wisdom. This gigantic life sheltering life-force continues to grow and grow, until death. It's staunch roots thrusted deep into the earth to sustain life. The roots of the tree are sometimes longer than the tree itself. And Oh, how it bends, never breaking as the leaves seem to sing to the sacred music of the wind. When I am laid to rest the song to the Notorious B.l.G., can you imagine that, fits me the best.

I am that tree. For God has blessed me to stretch out my two long, black arms like branches, and shelter many from harm. My seeds, he has willed to make multiply. Baring good fruits from a good sturdy tree. I am that tree. My roots are brawny, they run deep in the veins of my children, and their children, and my children's children. For they, my children, are what I truly live for. To see the Keys Group legacy continued, guided by the right hand of God down every path.

I've known storms. To keep from perishing, I had to bend. Bending, stretching, often until my very roots cracked, but never have I been broken.

Now, here I stand, big, Black, and proud, forever absorbing, growing, changing, until the day I die.

Go onward Keys Kids, continue the legacy, but take heed, keep the will of God in your eyes, in your souls, and in your hearts, and God will always be right by your side willing to help you in times of strife.

If I could express my feelings in colors, oh how magnificent that would be! My colors of life so vivid as you see them rushing into the burning blue heavens above your head, and suddenly explode into a barrage of shimmering splendor, this is how I feel. The spirit is working through me.

The Deity has laid a blessing on me. He has truly shown me. The finest, most precious gift you can ever hope to give cannot be bought, at any store, at any price. The finest gift that I can give to you is kindness! Kindness! KINDNESS! Simple isn't it? Yet, this simple, free act is the most lacking in the world.

There is a callousness, a cold hearted chill that breathes on society. Look around you, people pushing and shoving, as they rush pass you. For the most part, not as much as a howdy do!

As you have seen business is tough. Good people fail as well as bad people. Try to surround yourself with good, spirit-filled people...whoever they are. Get as much education and experience as you can. Ask to be a free Intern. Yes, work for free if you get a chance to LEARN the profession.

Education, knowledge, money, and preparation, these are all-important ingredients to success. However, I believe the two *most* important ingredients are Faith and Perseverance. Don't give up...just don't give up. Dream and have absolute faith that your dream will come true. God cannot help you unless you create an atmosphere for Him to help. Faith is the atmosphere —perseverance is the action.

It will soon be time for the "Bird Heads" to take over my companies. Incidentally, I call my kids "Bird Heads"...and it's amazing that they call their kids the same thing. Anyway, it will soon be time for them to take over and make Keys Group work. I hope they understand that unless they operate within the blessing bestowed upon our Keys Group Companies, they will experience difficulties they just can't handle.

To all of you who read this, please don't think I am a religious freak...believe me, I am far from that. I have sins of my father I am not able to dump anywhere. I am a bigger sinner than most of you who read this. However, God will forgive you as often as you ask.

I give special thanks to my wife Anna, who has stuck with me from the very beginning of my athletic career and my business career. A.C. Franklin, my mother, you are ill with Parkinson and may not be able to read this. However, your spirit speaks to me and I know you are pleased with this book. It captures the essence of a mother's prayers for her only son. I love you and I will be there for you until my last breath...even as your grandkids lose their blessings and long life as they fail in their duties to you. Thank you for the blessings you gave me that we all inhaled...goodbye.

Brady Keys, Jr.

158

Brady Keys' Journey To A Dream

by Mylitta Brown

Employee of KAB, to Brady on his 30th Anniversary

If you could envision a dream, it happened in 1967. It was a prayer answered and it came from heaven. I'll serve All-Pro Chicken, they'll love it. The customers will be all mine.

Then came my next answered prayer in 1969. A Burger King Franchise in Michigan you see, I believed again and my family believed in me.

•1970 — A Manpower Training School appeared and I marched on and gained business power with no fear. Over the next two years I grew in Power. My businesses shot up just like the tower. Six KFC's, 30 All-Pro Chicken stores, and wait, I just started, there's more. I also opened a game machine business for fun, but that wasn't it, I wasn't done.

•1973 — All-Pro Chicken was sold, but wait the rest of the story has yet to be told.

•1977 — I sold the game machine in Pittsburgh for one in Detroit you see. It was just another business move for me.

•1981 — A hair salon Ramsey & Ramsey, I'd just begun.

•1982 — I did a business trade and it was the right thing to do.

•1987 — God answered another prayer, and yes it came from Heaven. For a small fee Community Access News was founded and people would learn what CAN really means.

•1988 — It was time to set it straight, I expanded to twelve Burger King Operations that Detroit would come to find, but in 1990, I sold them because I had other things in mind.

•1991 — The fun had just begun. I purchased WJIZ FM Radio Station in Georgia and I would play the best music for you.

•1992 — It was the start of something new. I opened Keys

News & Gift Shop on June 27th and GOD answered another prayer for me.

•1993 — WJYZ AM Radio Station would come to be.

•1994 — The stars were shooting and I soared. I founded All-Pro Ostrich Ranch in Albany. It's the best tasting meat in all of the world and even the President has come to agree.

•1995 — Was the time to make things really come alive. The First Annual Black Business Directory was published and sold because by that time other black businesses and all I had done needed to be told.

So, here I am in 1997 with all this history in my file and all I can do is think back, thank God, and just smile. It's been 30 years of excellence but I'm truly not done. Look out world because the Keys Journey has just begun.

Historical Photos

Colonel Sanders makes his first visit to an American inner city area. He visits Brady and family in Detroit.

Colonel, Brady, Anna, and Sons Rodney and Jamie in front of one of Brady's Restaurants.

The Colonel celebrates his birthday with Brady and his wife Anna.

Brady was the pioneer for all fast food operators. However, the "fall out" from his efforts caused businesses like *Essence* to get started. Once Brady was in any position of power he helped small businesses to get contracts with Burger King and KFC like Greene Herman and Associates. Most notable was and is even today, Byron Lewis and Uniworld Advertising Agency.

Brady has a lot of help, but Jesse Jackson and PUSH have to rank at the top. Brady's conflicts with Burger King and KFC are enough to write an entire book. Jesse helped stop Burger King from taking the stores after President Nixon created the opportunity for Brady to "borrow" $2.5 million to build them. They stopped KFC from taking them when Brady got behind on his payments to them. Brady returned the favor by being a heavy donor to Jesse's Campaign for President and publicly supporting him in a hostile southern environment. The white dominated South still stings Brady for things like that.

Congressman Sanford Bishop presents Brady with A Congressional Award.

Brady watches as a Gun is destroyed in one of his three Gun Buy Backs. Two in Georgia and one in Florida.

Brady and Rev. Jesse Jackson teamed up to bring the Harlem Globe Trotters to Albany, Ga. Jesse is one of Brady's favorite people and they have teamed up many times to deal with corporate adversaries.

Milt Sanders KFC Franchisee in Tifton teams with Brady to sponsor one of BKFC's Christmas tournaments, which BKFC has sponsored for 11 straight years.

Adrienne Archie, Editor of Black Business Directory and Community Access News with Representative Winfred Dukes who is in the BBD as a contractor.

Don Murtugh, Franchise Representative of KFC Corporation presents Brady his 20 year plaque and pin. Brady is in line for his 30 year award now.

Jim Fowler, Wild Animal Trainer & Today Show TV Personality on the air at WJIZ.

Brady receiving the award for #1 Urban Contemporary Station in the Nation.

A.C. with her Blessed son Brady at a BKFC awards party in 1990.

Royal Hannaford Brothers Circus visit to Albany was sponsored by Brady Keys KFC. Jay the Clown clowns around with BKFC Managers.

The Ostrich Business was a great love for Brady and family. God was not consulted neither was it blessed.

Brady & Maxine Willis created Kids Enjoy Yourself Without Drugs (K.E.Y.S.) which with the help of Danszar "De" Dinosuar, has helped, and is helping thousands to not do drugs.

Brady and his first franchised All-Pro Chicken with his two kids Rodney and Buzzy Keys showing off their new gloves.

Photos

Colorado State University Hall of Fame running back, Brady Keys, Jr., showing his cutting ability.

Brady in the heat of a National Football League game on the field St. Louis Cardinals vs. Dallas Cowboys.

First Dollar earned by Brady's first Restaurant January 27, 1967.

Brady's school, Urban Talent Development, founded by the Scoife family was awarded the SBA's highest honor for independent schools.

Mom A.C. with grandson Jamie at the ballfield.

Danny Rooney, President of Steelers with Anna and Brady in Steeler's office in Pittsburgh, Pennsylvania.

Great friends Alma (left) and Billy Nobles (third from right) really werer great friends when I moved to Albany and remain great friends to this day.

Phil Handy, business associate and great friend of Brady's with his family.

Brady III, Jamie, Doris (sister-in-law), Anna (wife) Rodney & Brady Tyrone all watch the ball.

Brady and the world reknown Honduran Herbalist Dr. Sebi at Keys Group Building.

President Nelson Mandela and Brady Keys, Jr. meet in South Africa.

**Brady Keys Jr., and his friend Bill Cosby. Brady and Bill played
sandlot football together in Los Angeles.**

From the first book about Brady Keys, Jr.
Football to Finance

by the late Mr. Art Rooney,
Founder of the Pittsburgh Steelers

This is the era of the non-person, the anti-hero and the disenchantment of youth.

It is an era when Horatio Alger plots are as out-of-date as leather headgears.

Brady Keys grew up in this point in time and his early accomplishments give him extraordinary credentials for the future.

He spent his early years in Austin, Texas. He was poor and, as he puts it, "appeared to be just another one of the countless, nondescript black boys — doomed to a lifetime of emptiness, inside some ghetto."

After high school, he wandered aimlessly from job to job before joining the Eagle Rock semi-pro football team in Los Angeles. At the time, Keys apparently considered this a simple diversion in his purposeless life. Actually it provided the spark that sent him reaching for the moon.

His semi-pro play was so outstanding, especially in a scrimmage against the Los Angeles Rams, that scouts at that game convinced this young man that there was some worth in all the old assumptions and moralities.

He selected Colorado State as his school. But when he enrolled he was a few years older and wiser than his classmates. He made his mark both scholastically and athletically.

It is at this point in his life that I can speak with most knowledge. He played for the Pittsburgh Steelers. I am the owner of that team.

He gave us every ounce of his ability on the playing field and he was fair and realistic in his negotiations off the field. Perhaps his rag-tag early days gave him a better sense of values than most.

A great example of his playing ability came in 1963. Keys was a cornerback on the defensive unit. A great many experts

189

believe this is the most difficult defensive position in football. And when you make a mistake, you make it out in the open before God and usually some 50,000 fans.

In 1963, not one of the exceptional wide receivers in the National Football League caught a touchdown pass on Brady. Neither sports writers nor the fans keep any statistics on that kind of feat, but it is an exceptional statistic, especially in those pass-conscious days of the long bomb.

He used both confidence and ingenuity to psyche his enemies on the playing field. He attempted to take away their concentration by talking to them. It worked with a lot of folks, Keys once said, but never with Raymond Berry. Berry was the great Baltimore end that teamed up with Johnny Unitas to make life impossible for Brady Keys.

Today Brady Keys has become a successful businessman, a recognized leader not only in the black community but in the community PERIOD.

To help him along the way, Keys refers to the philosophy of William DuBois, a famed black intellectual and the patron saint of some of the more militant societies. Go into business, urged DuBois, in order to develop the wealth and power needed to change the black man's position in American society.

Brady Keys is trying.

ART ROONEY

November 27, 1970

190